I0507851

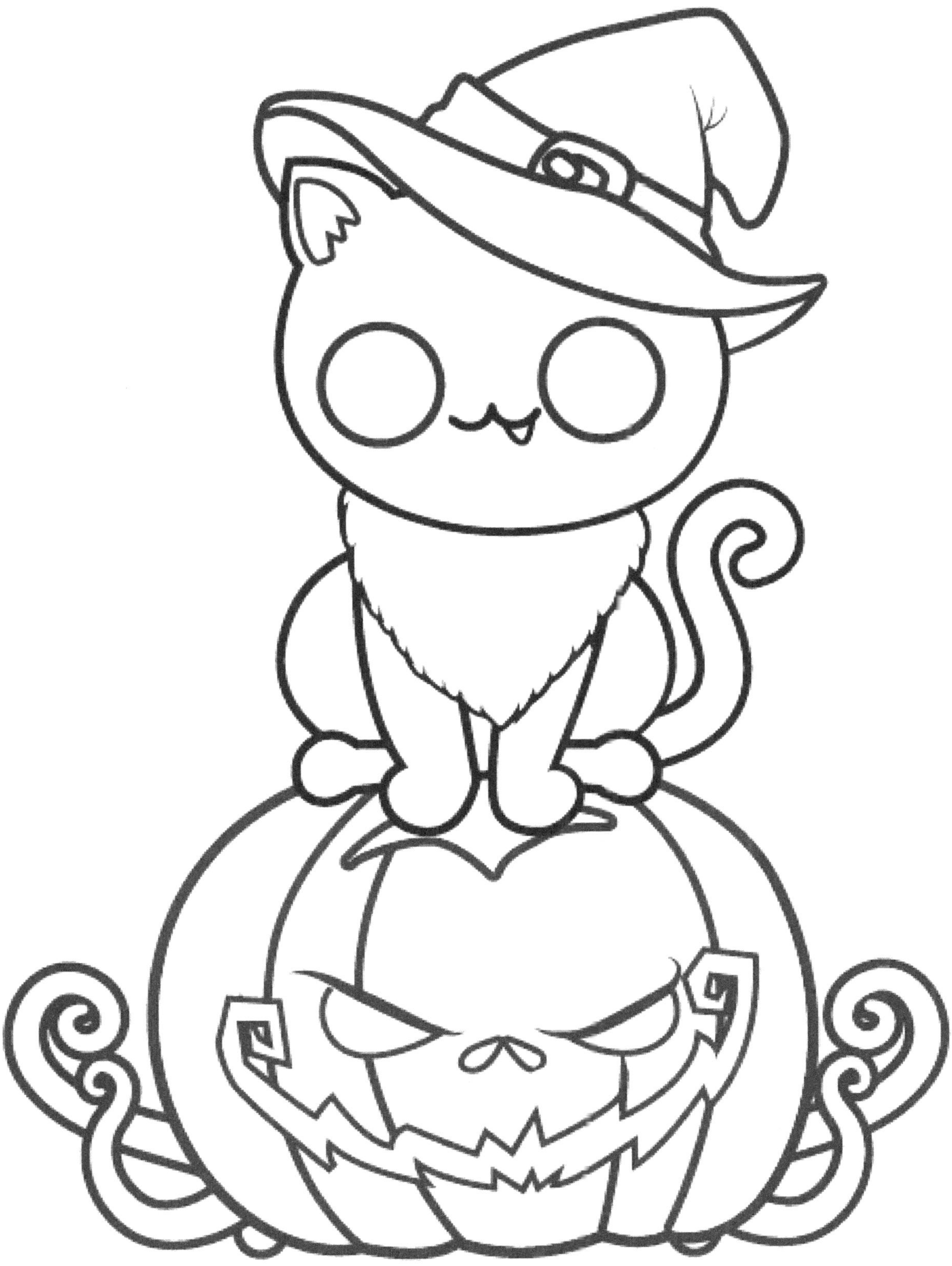

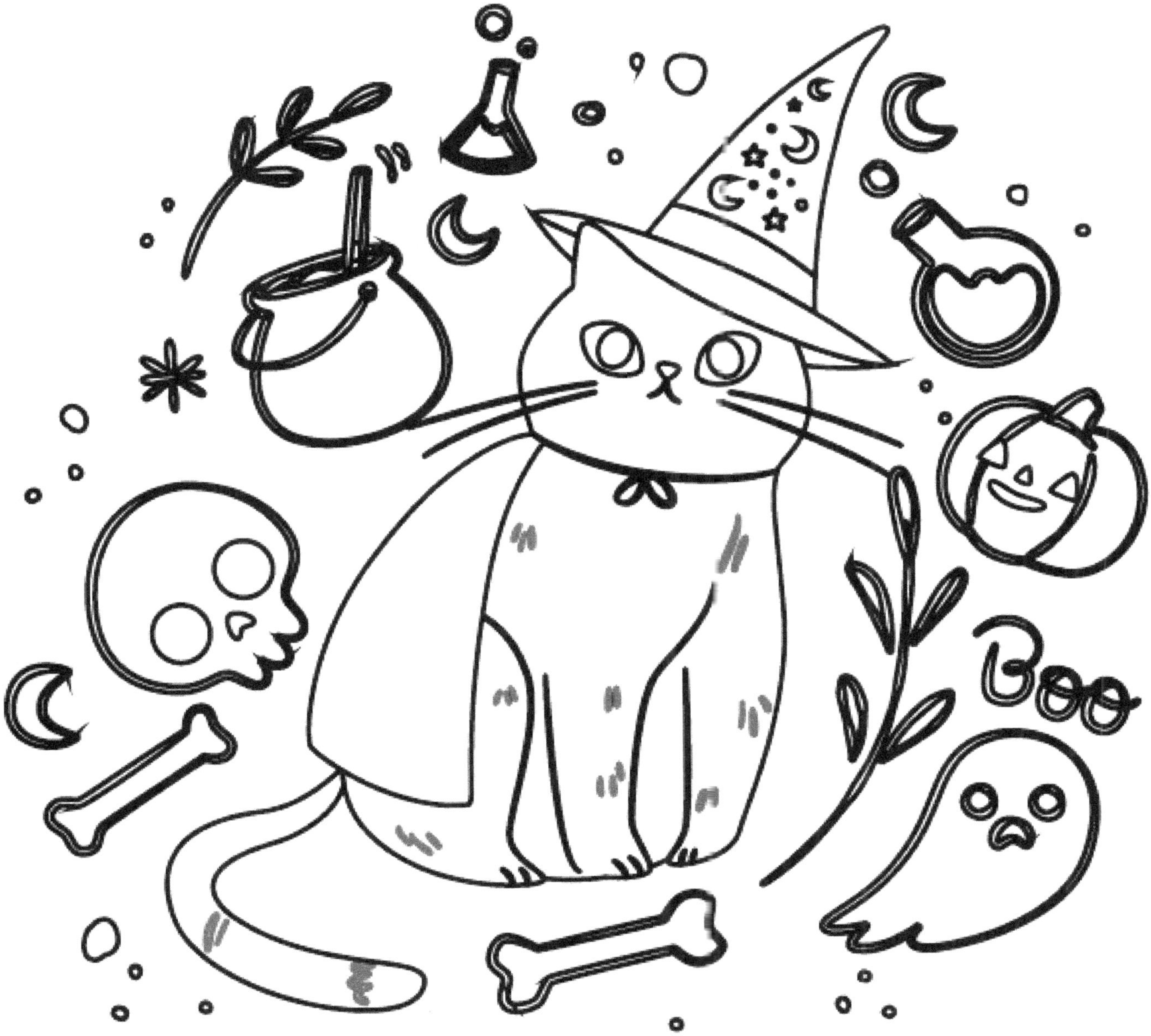
Boo

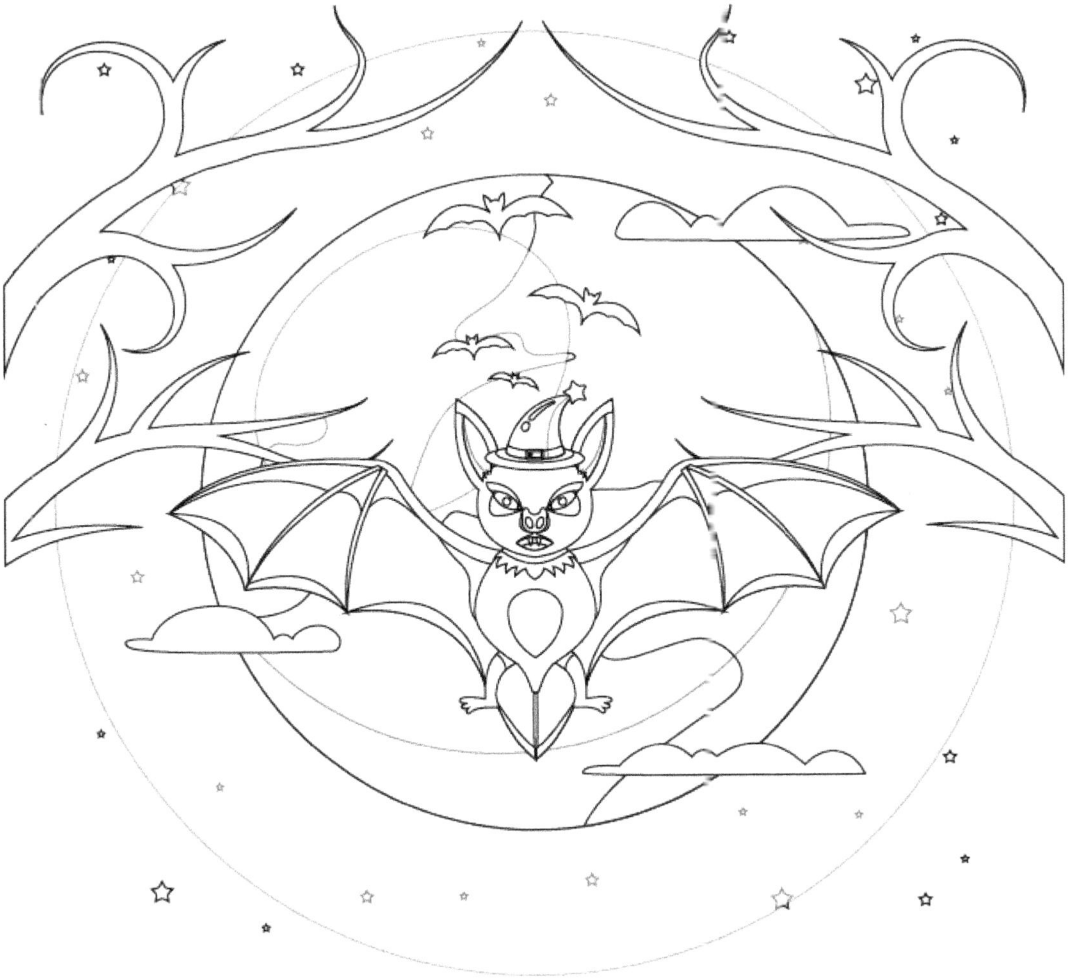

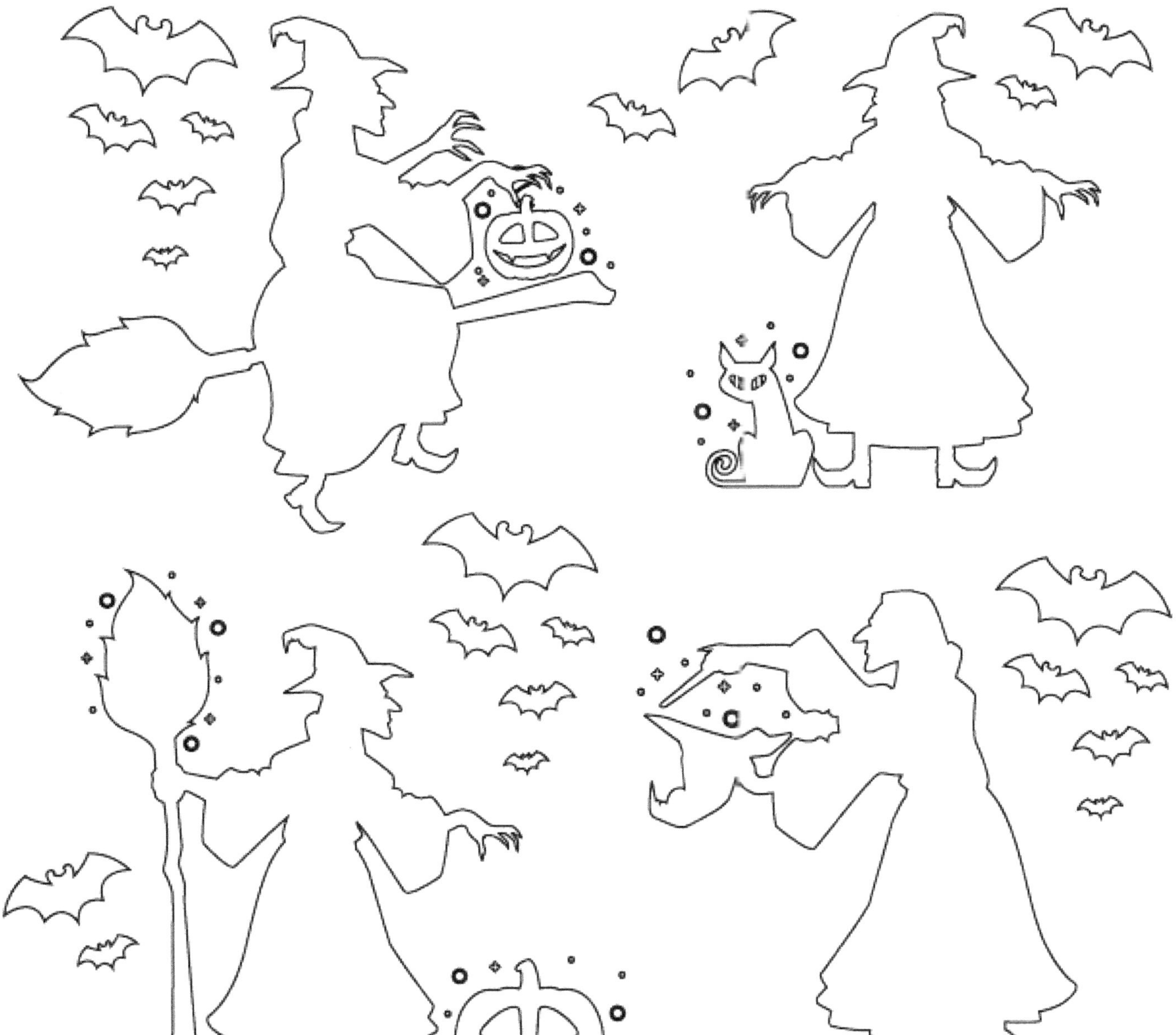

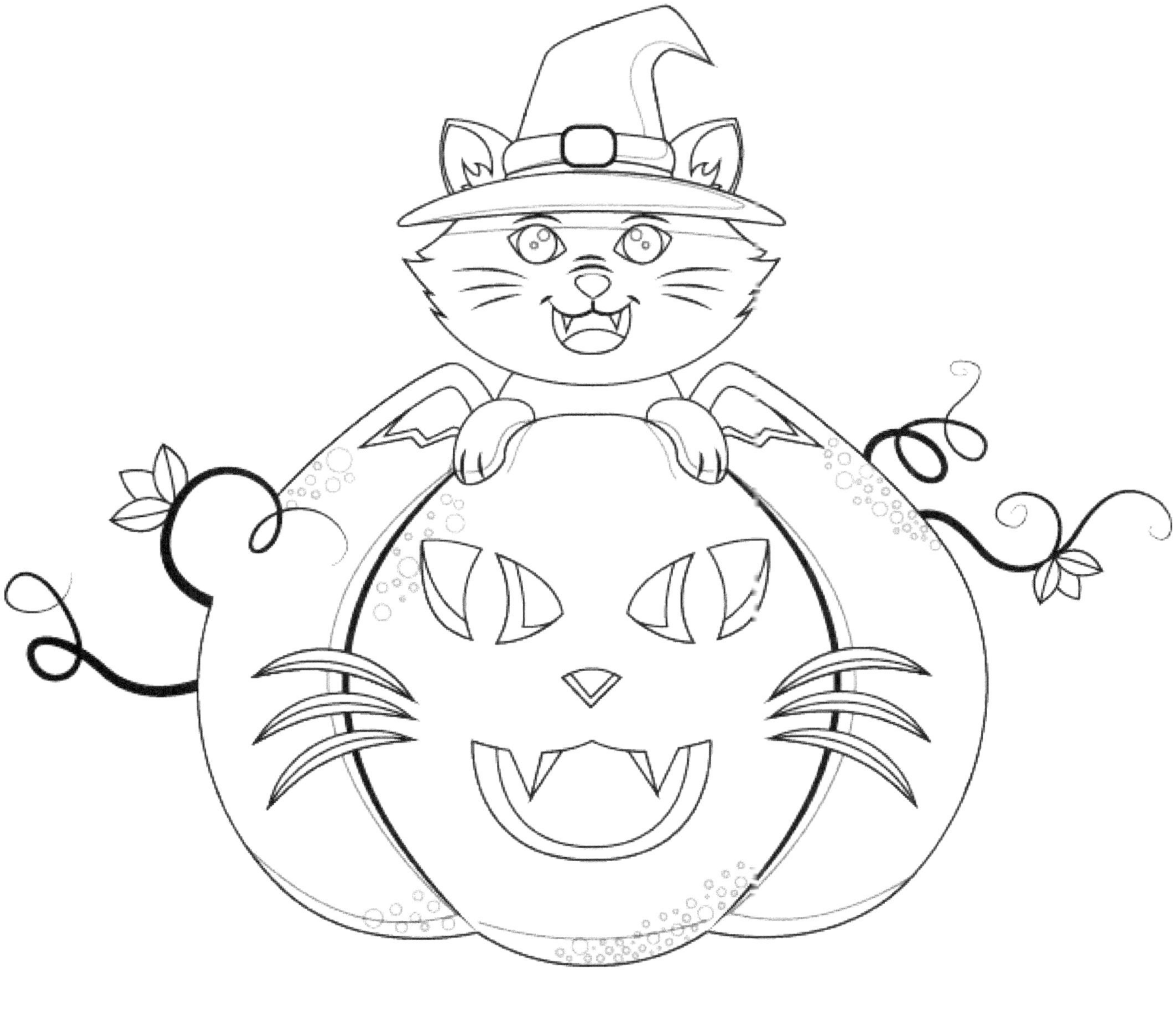

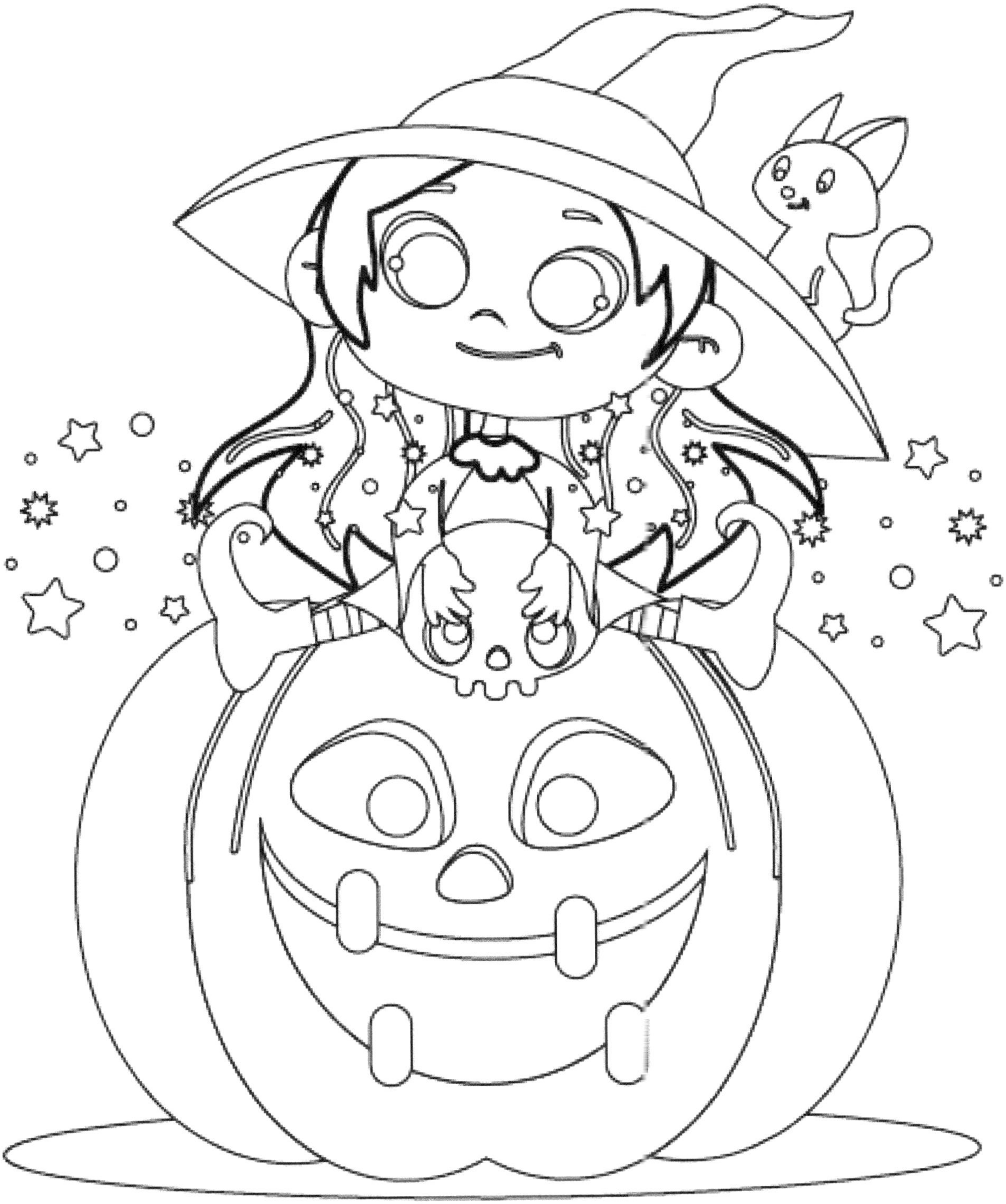

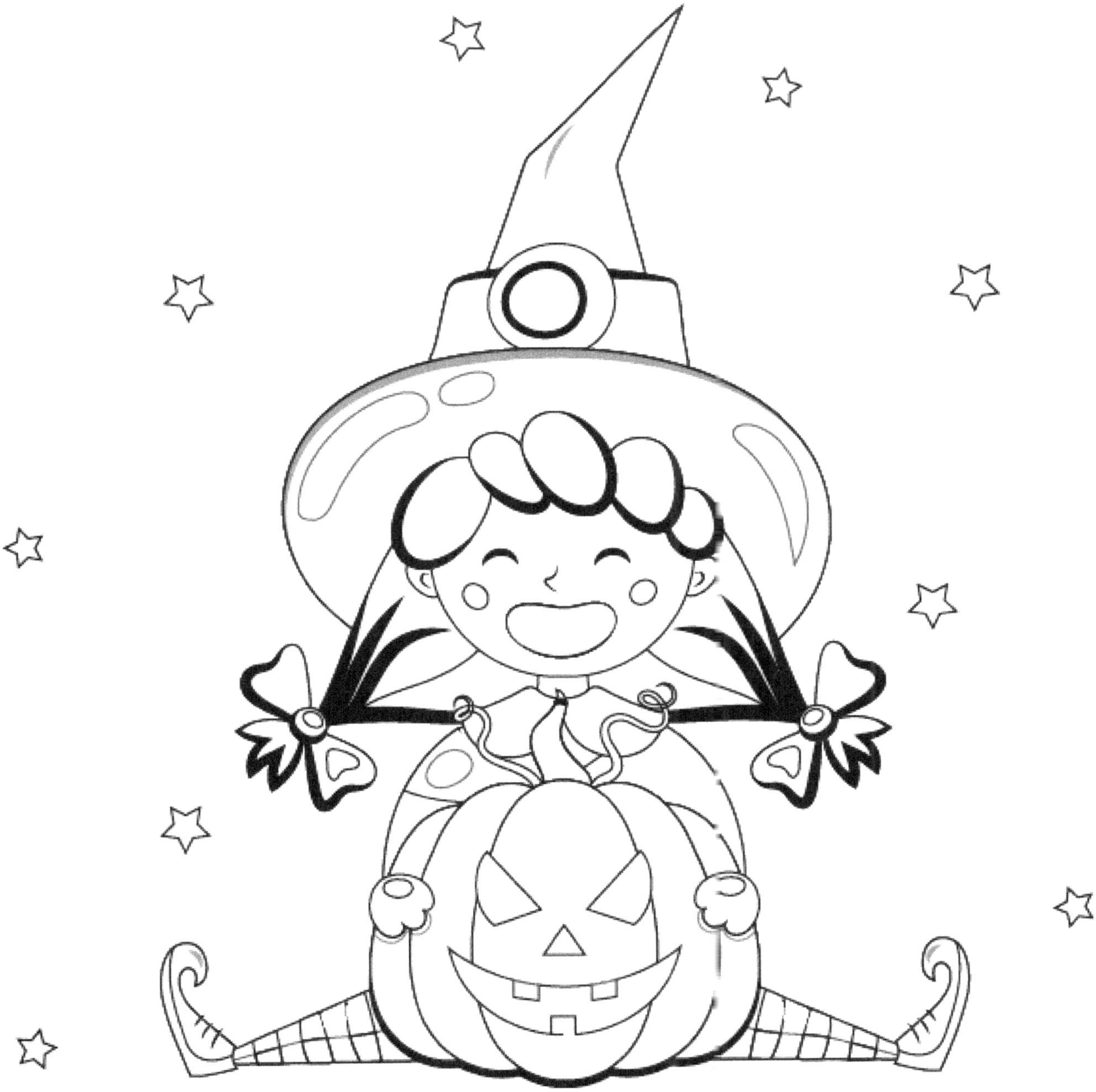

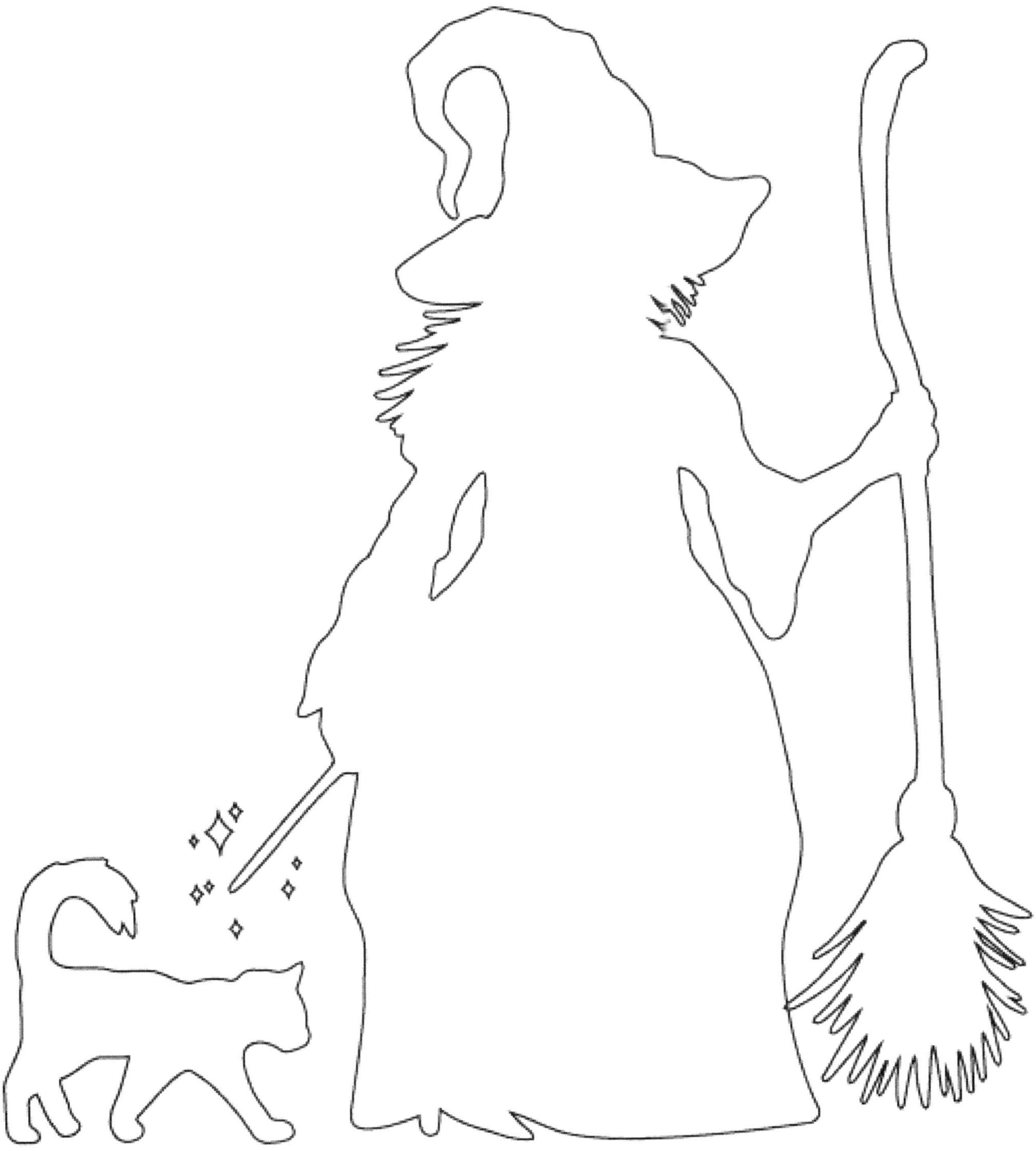

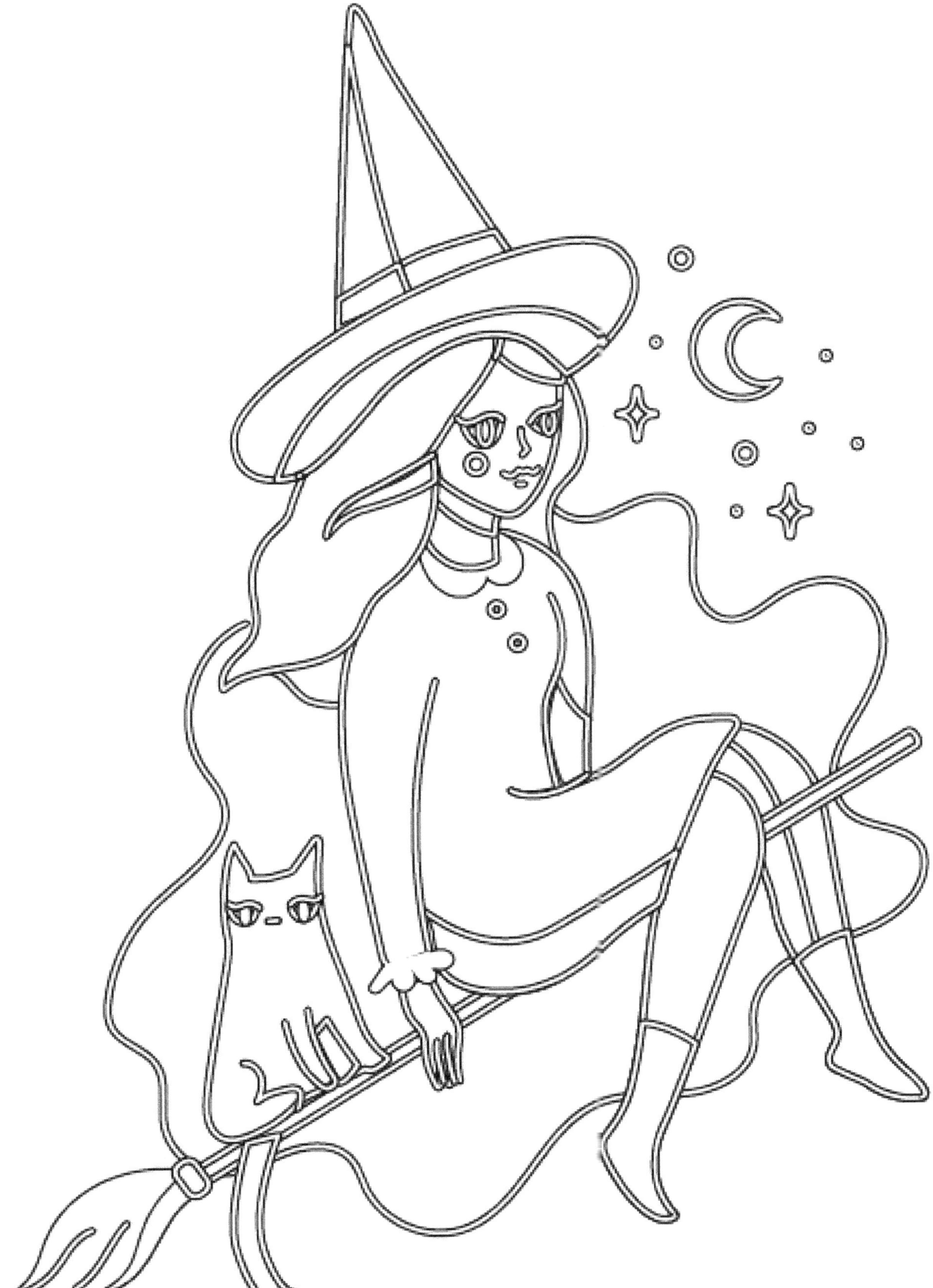

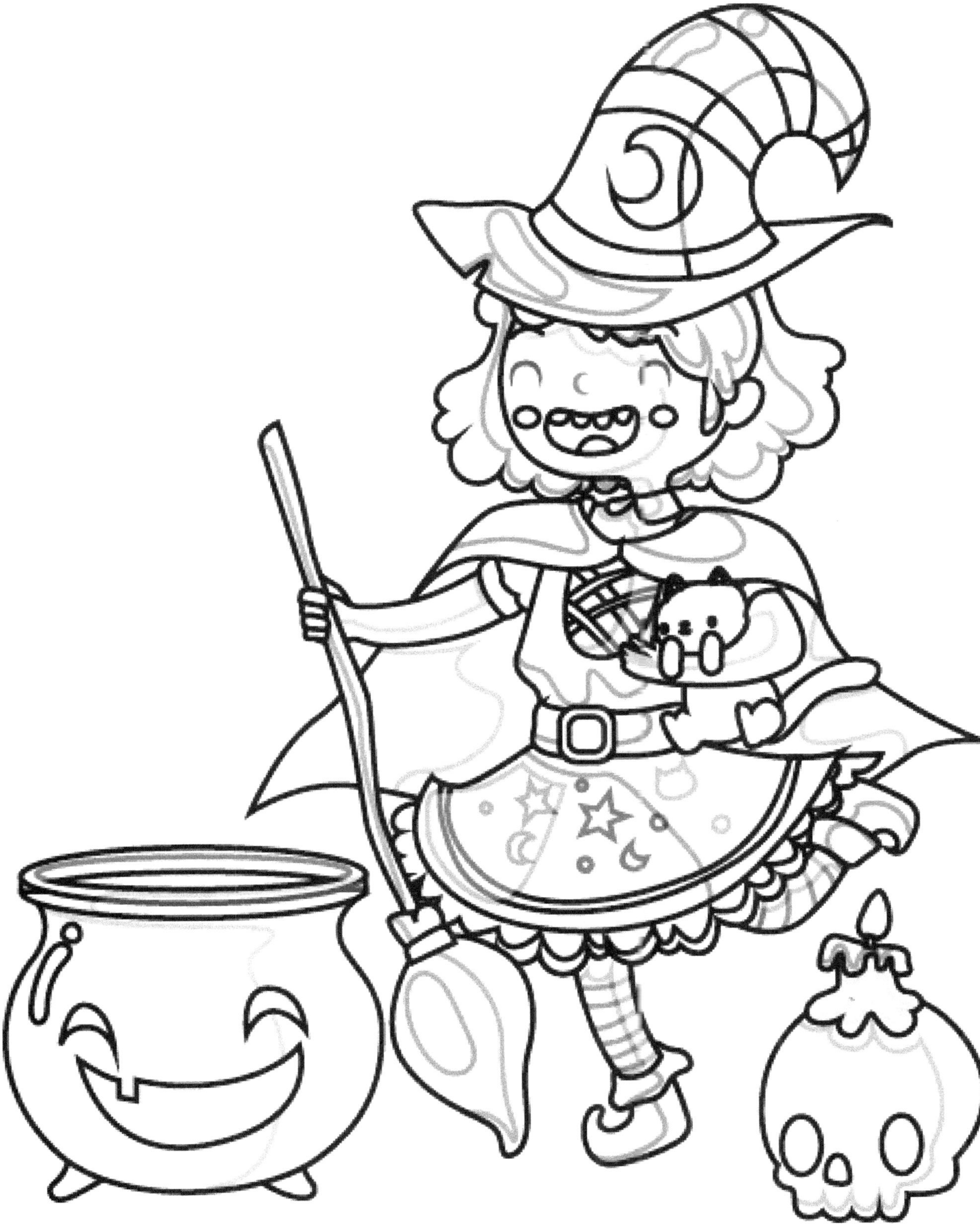

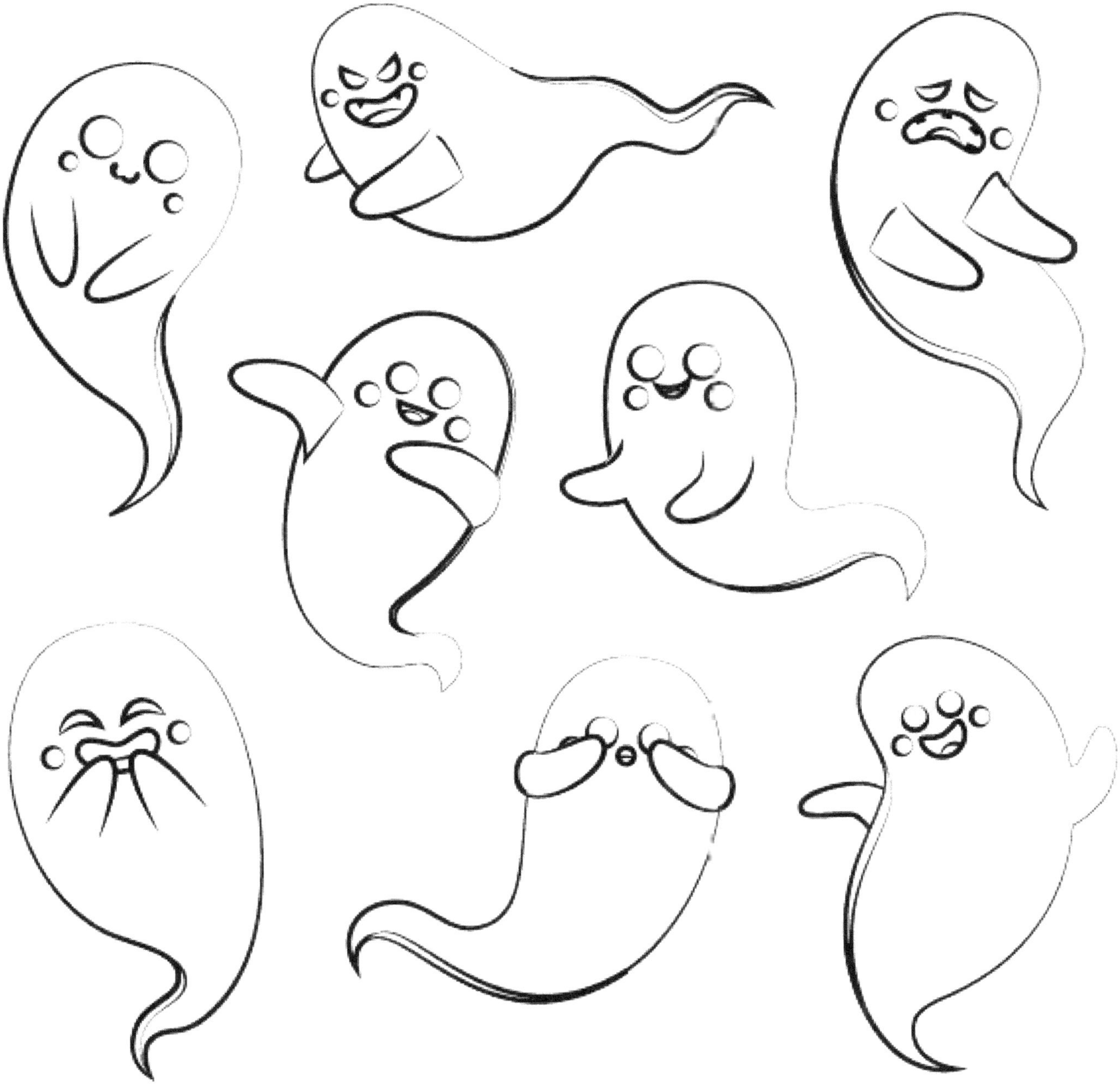

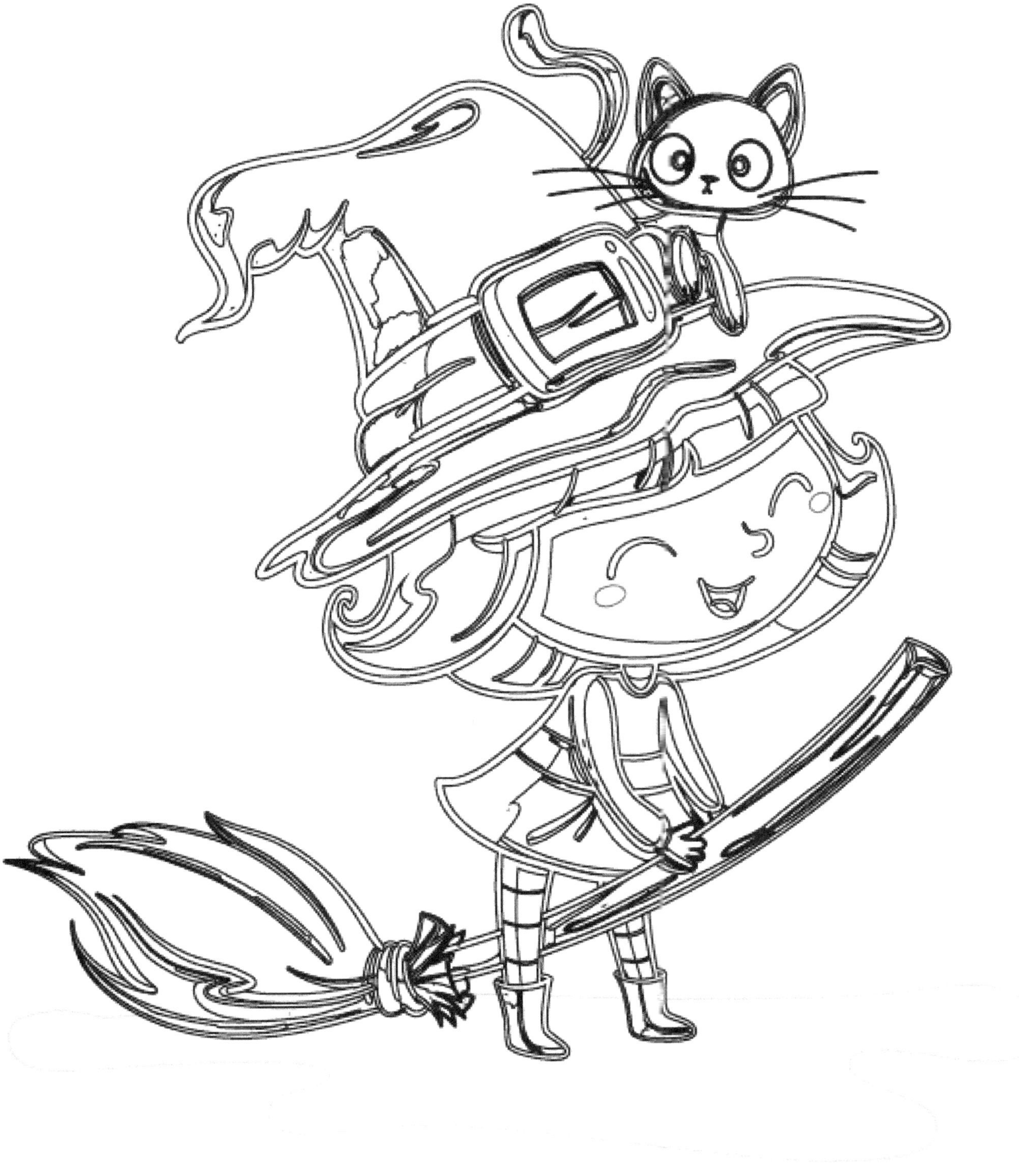

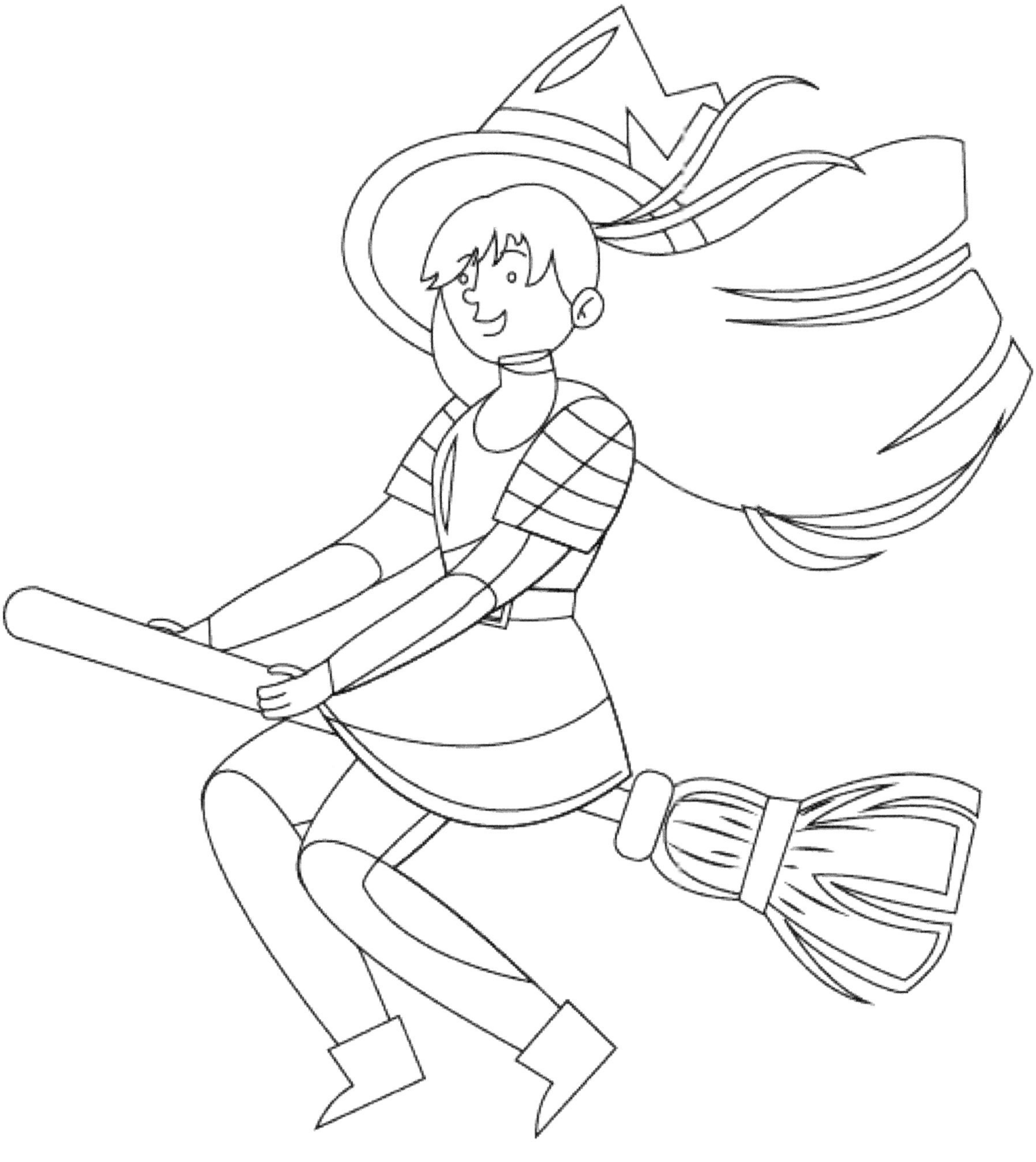

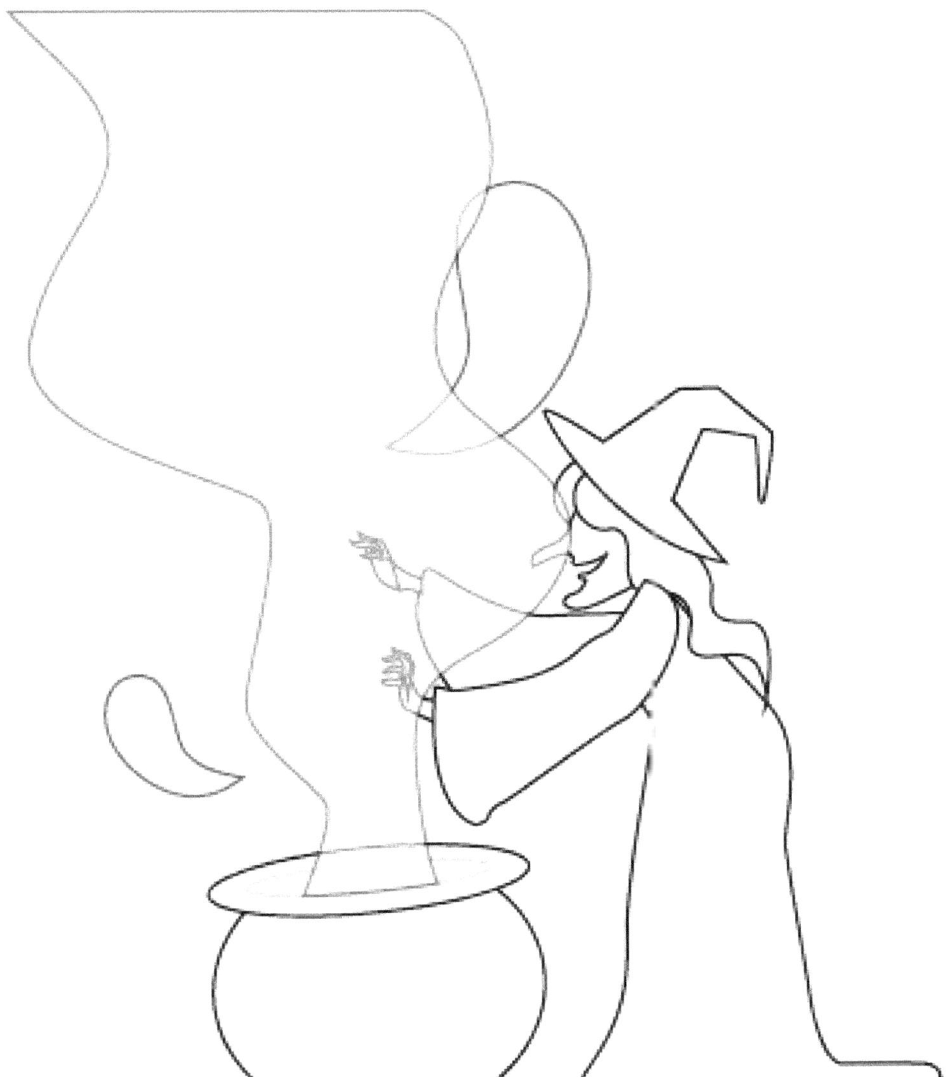

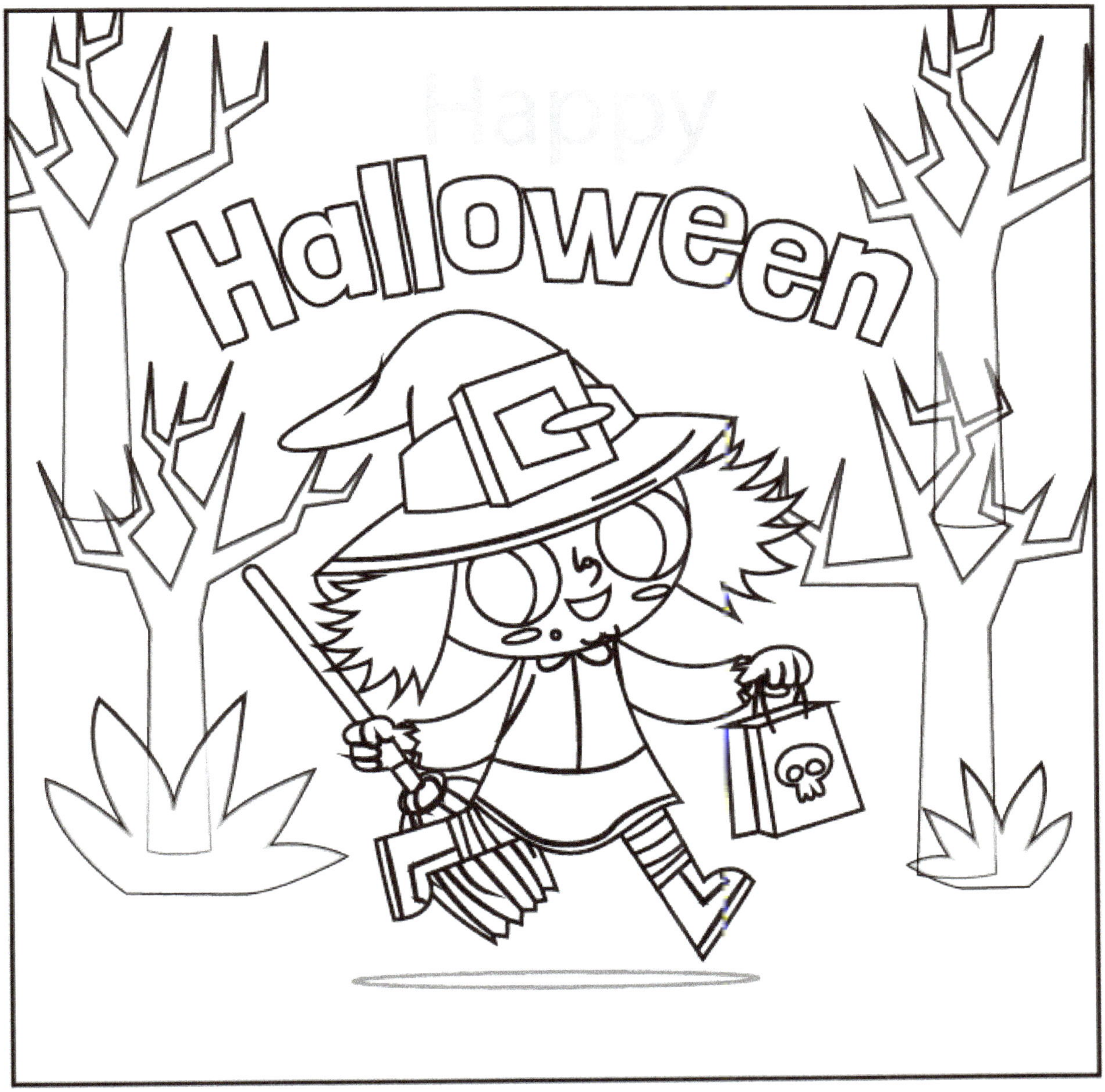
Happy
Halloween

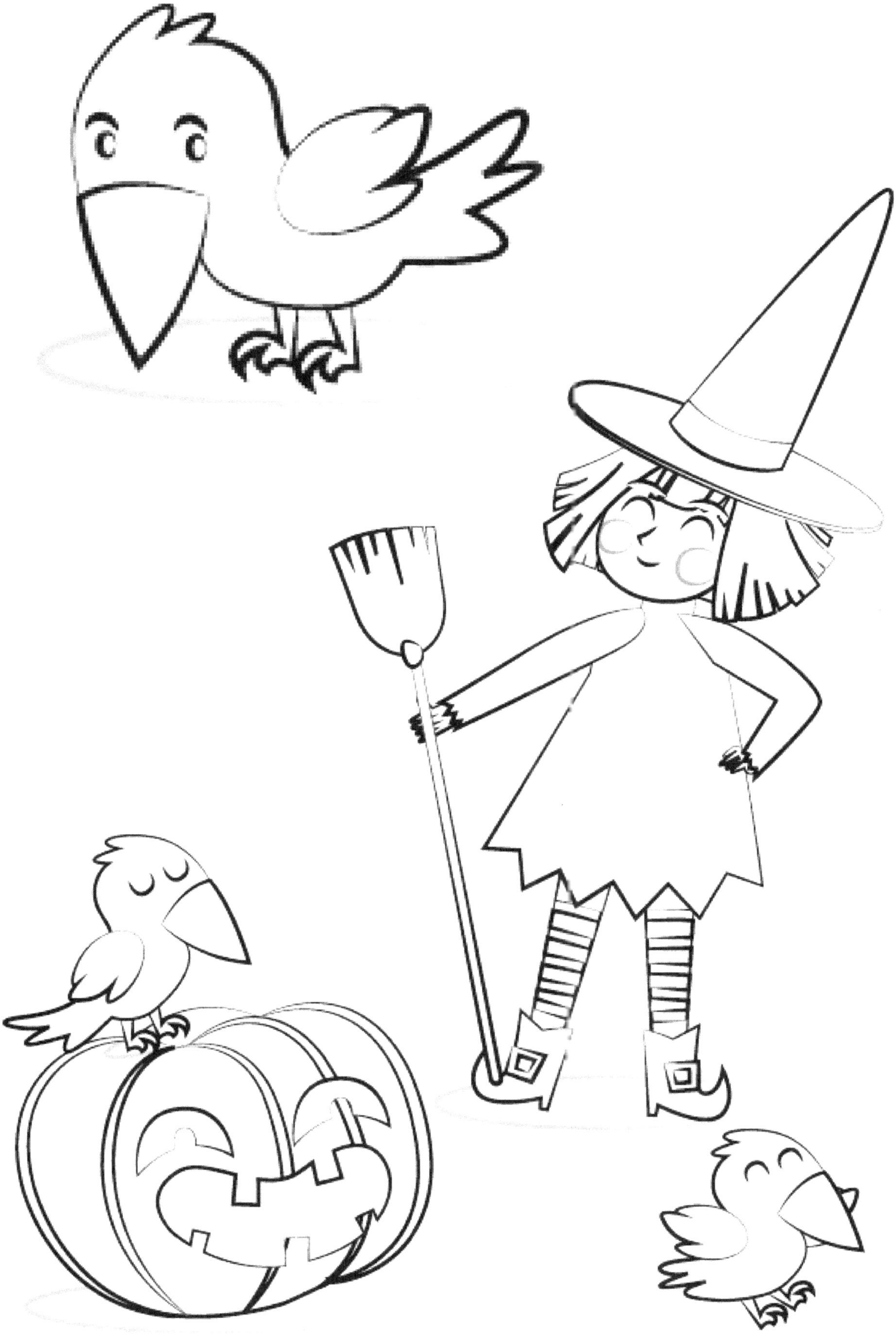

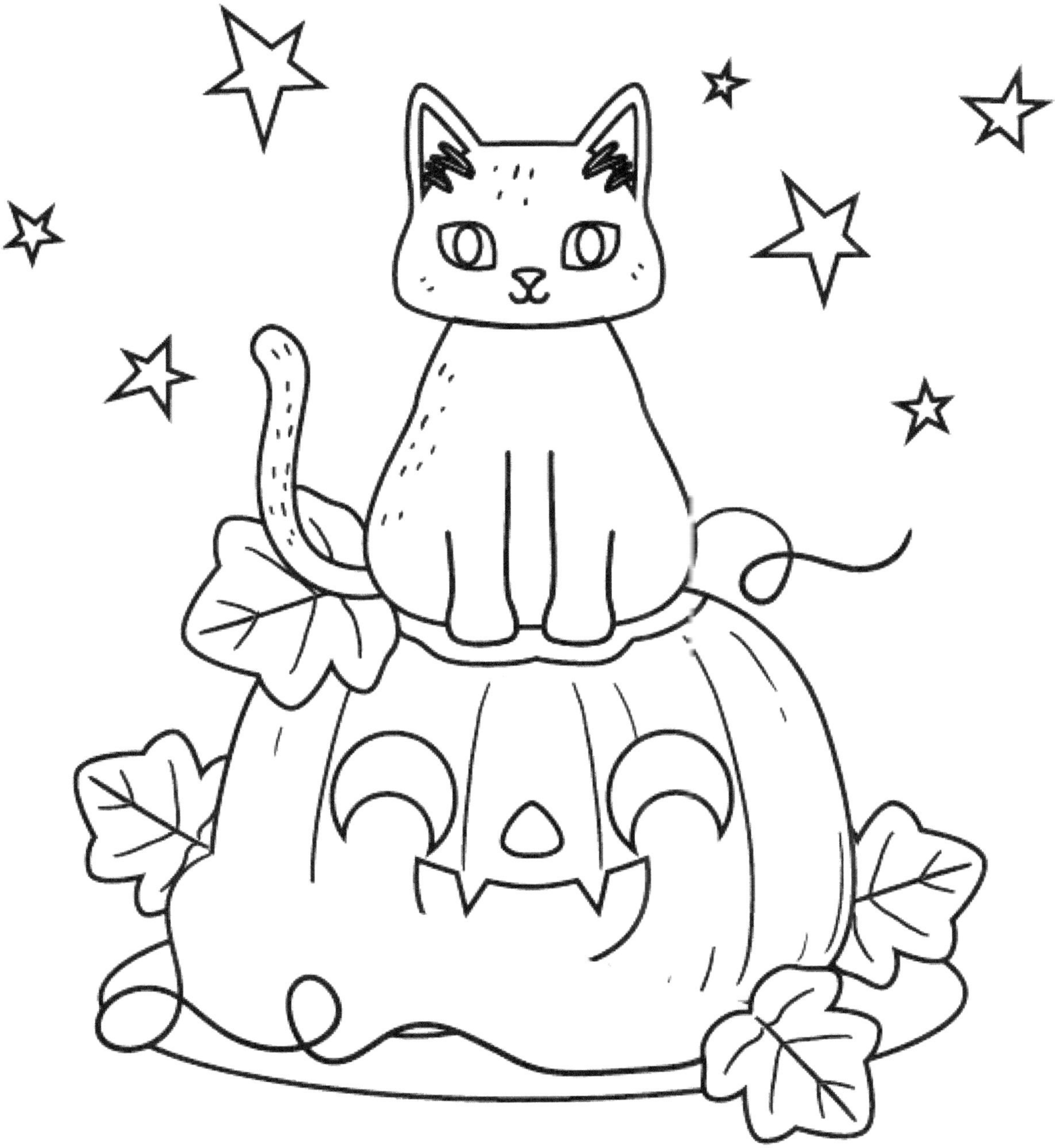

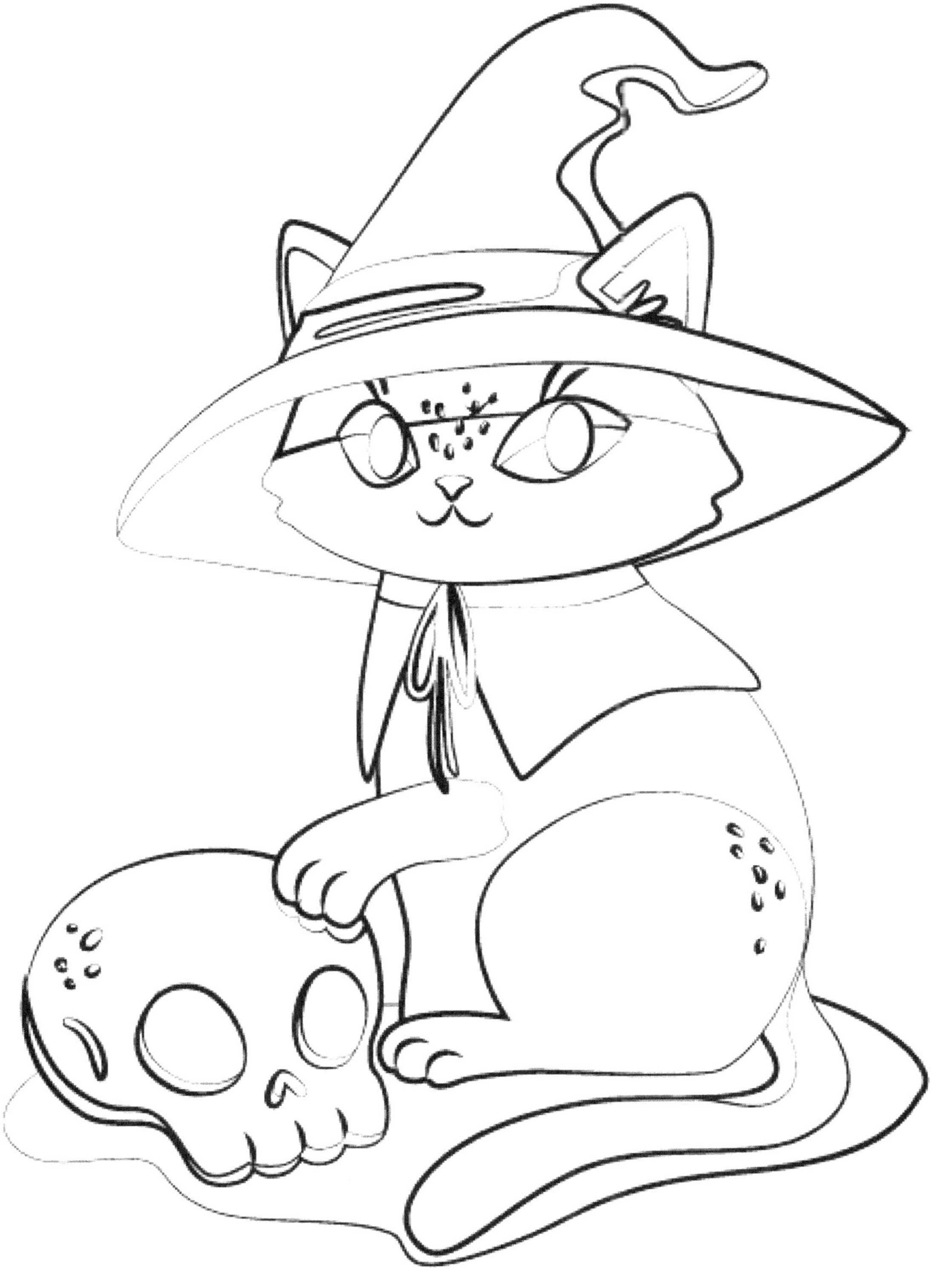

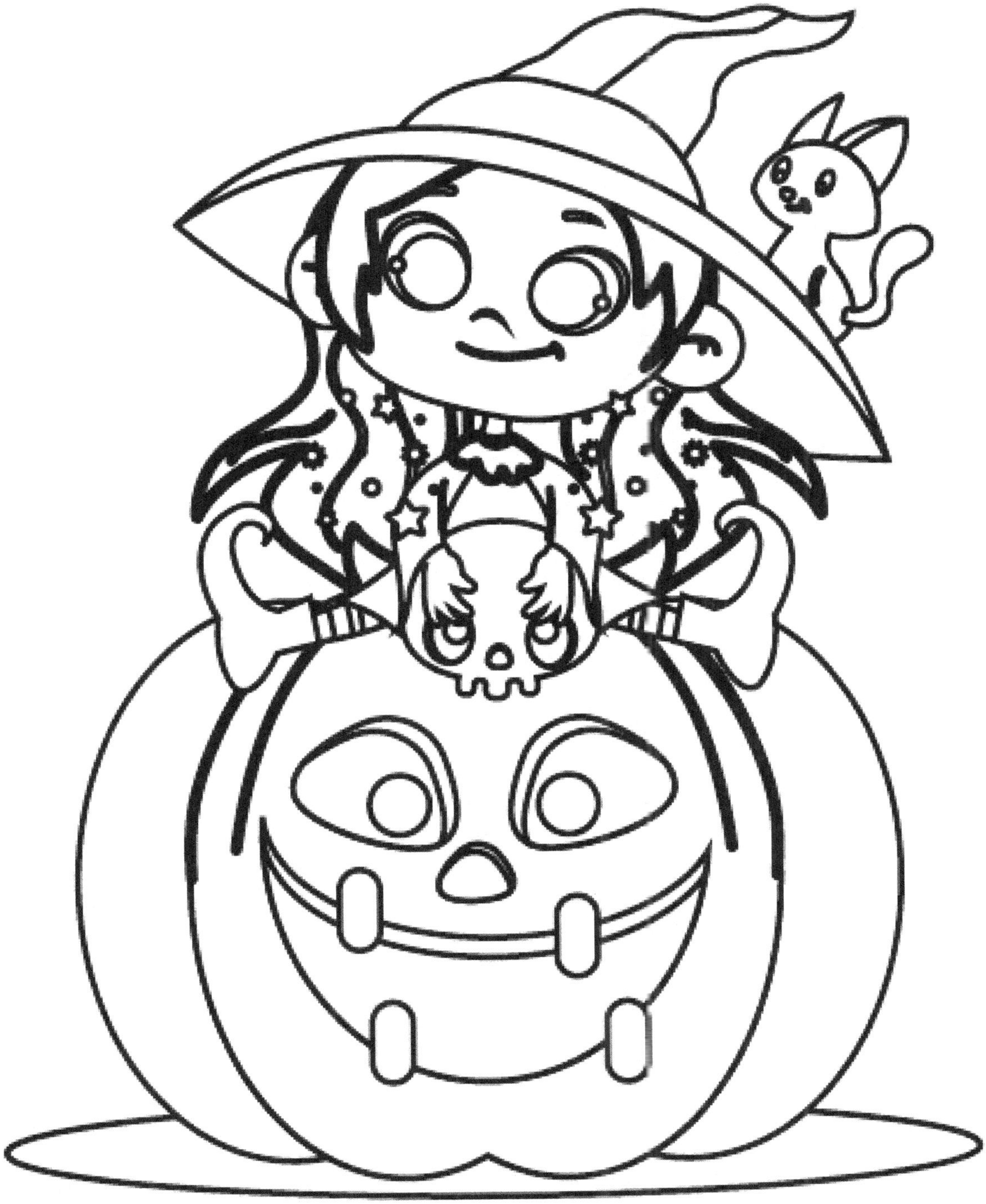

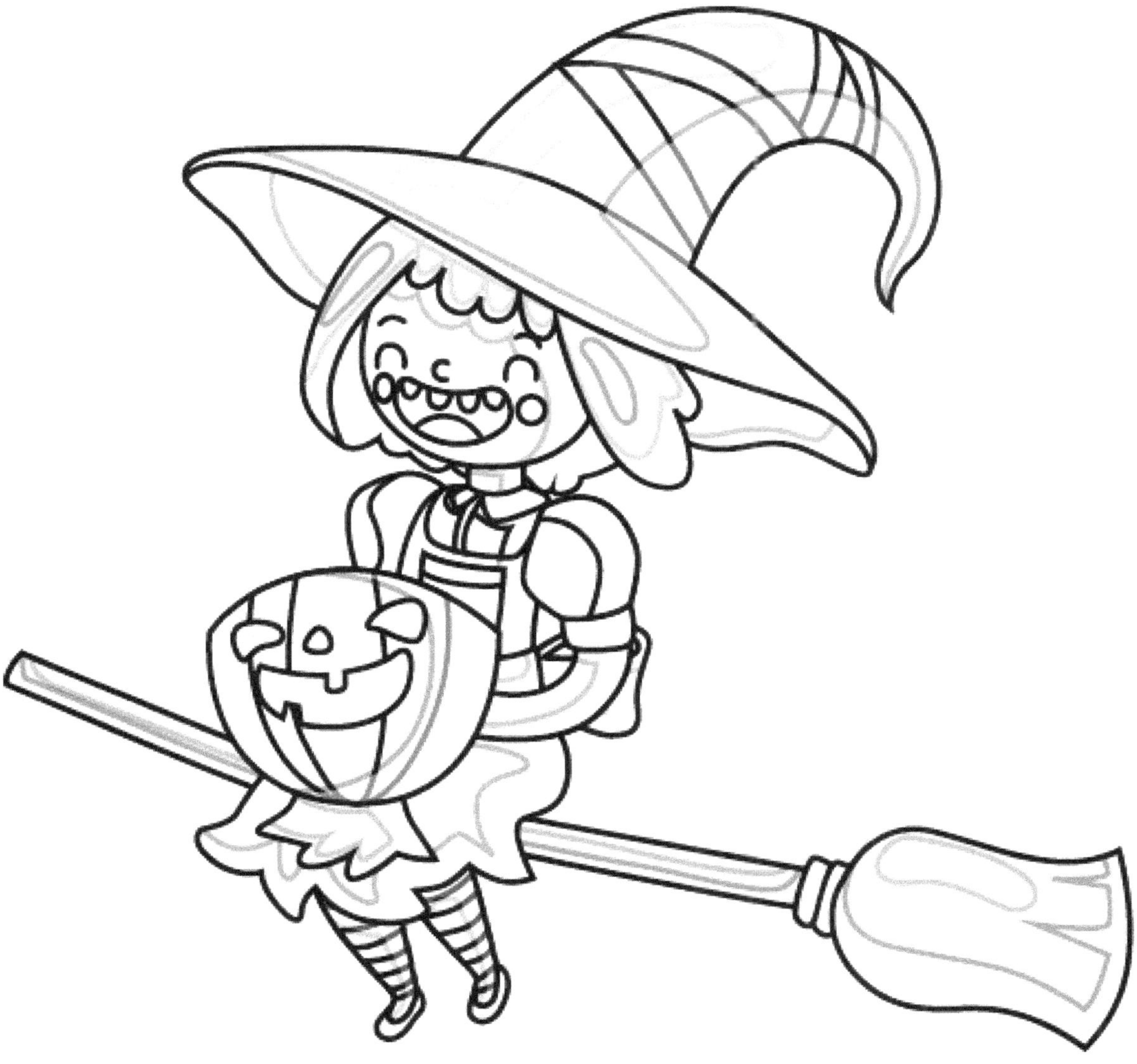

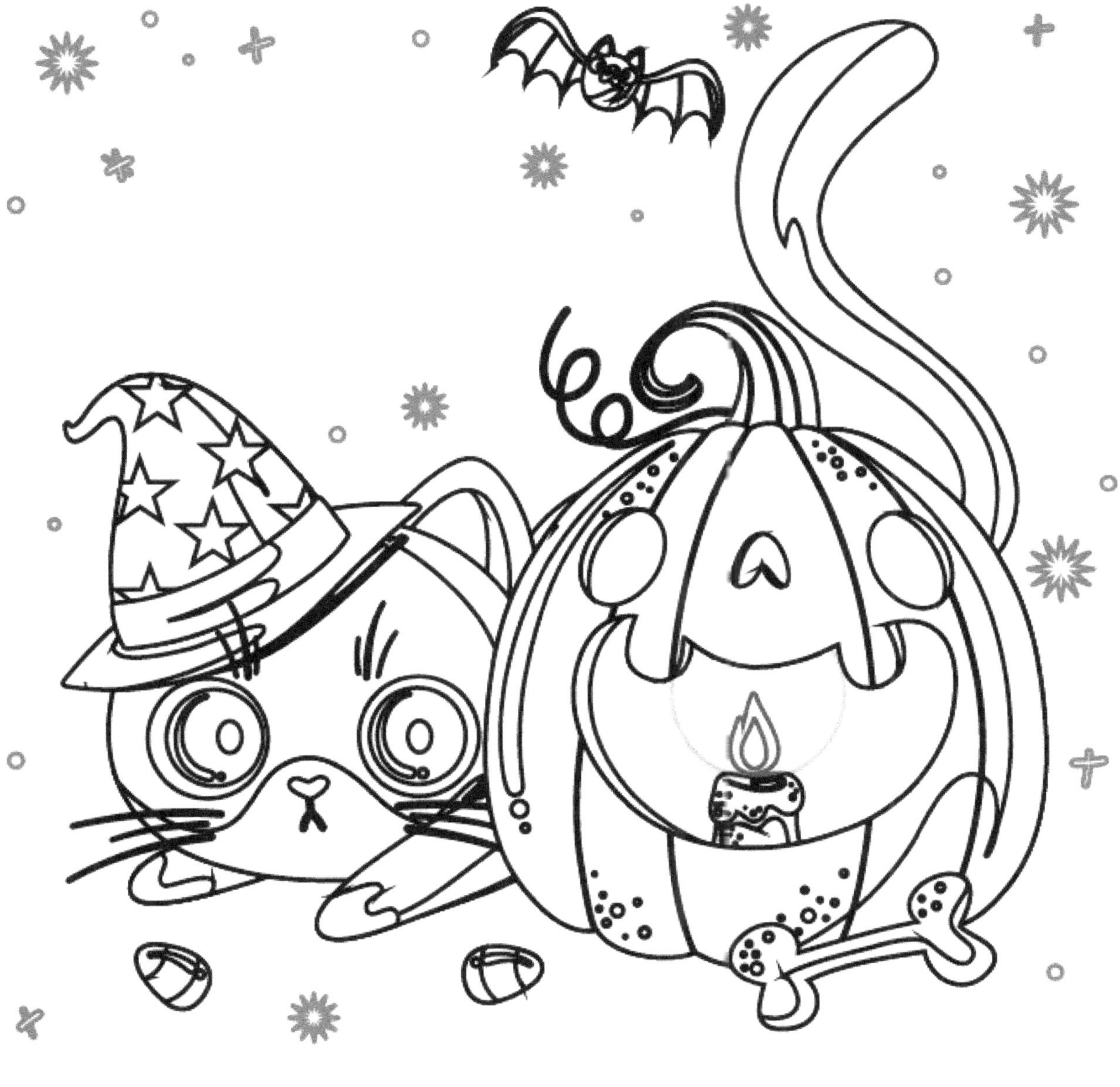

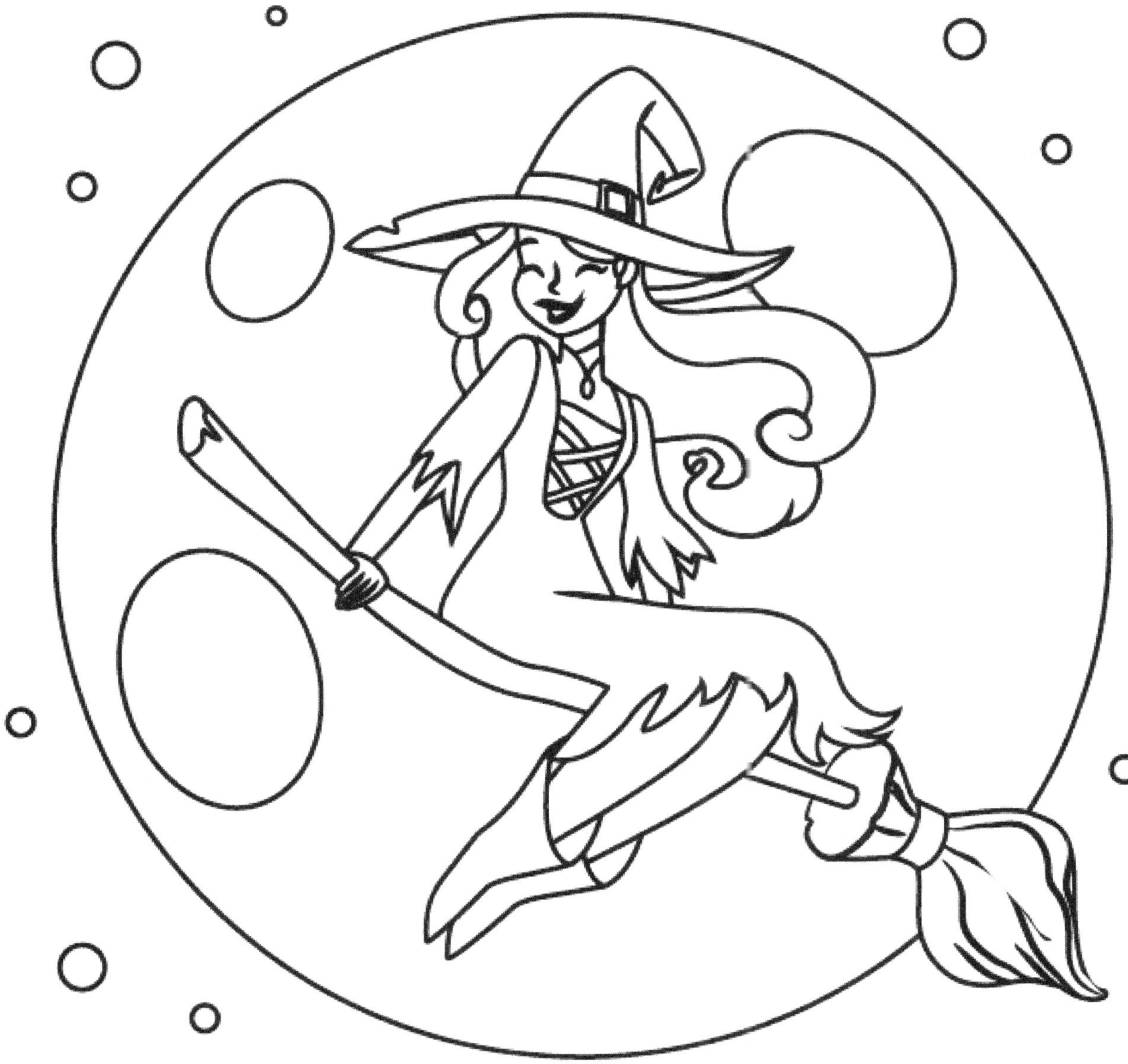

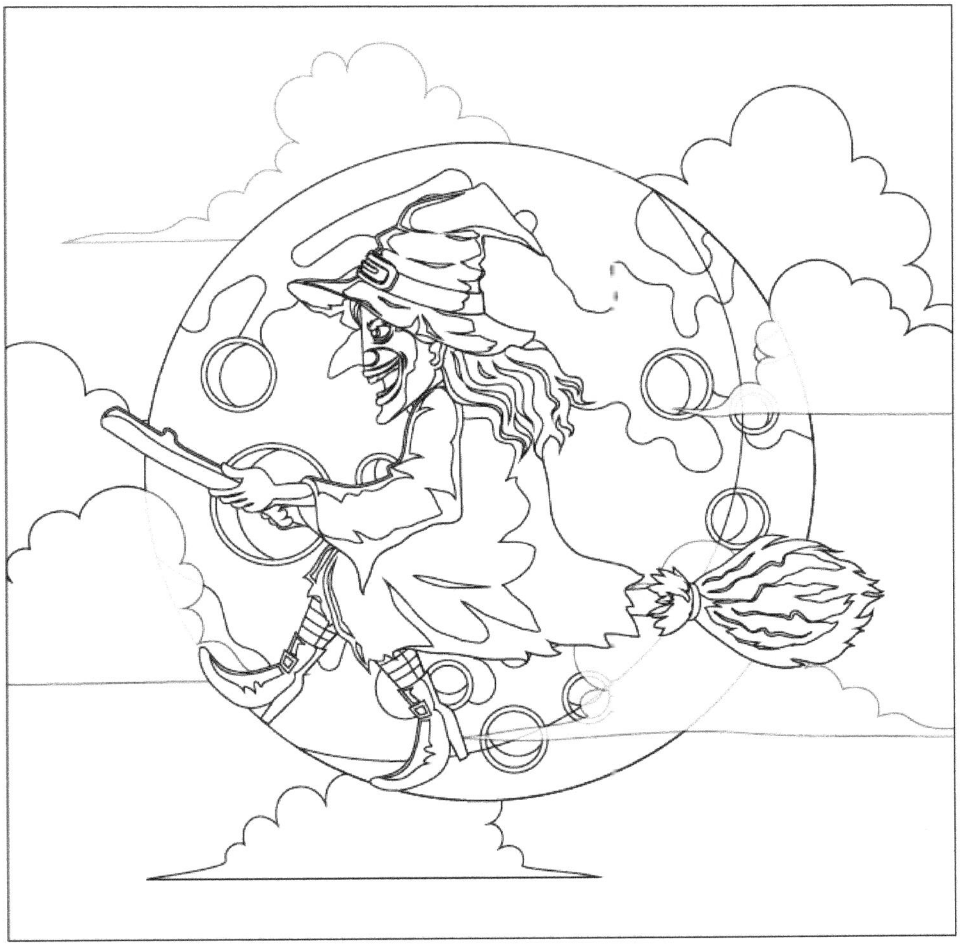

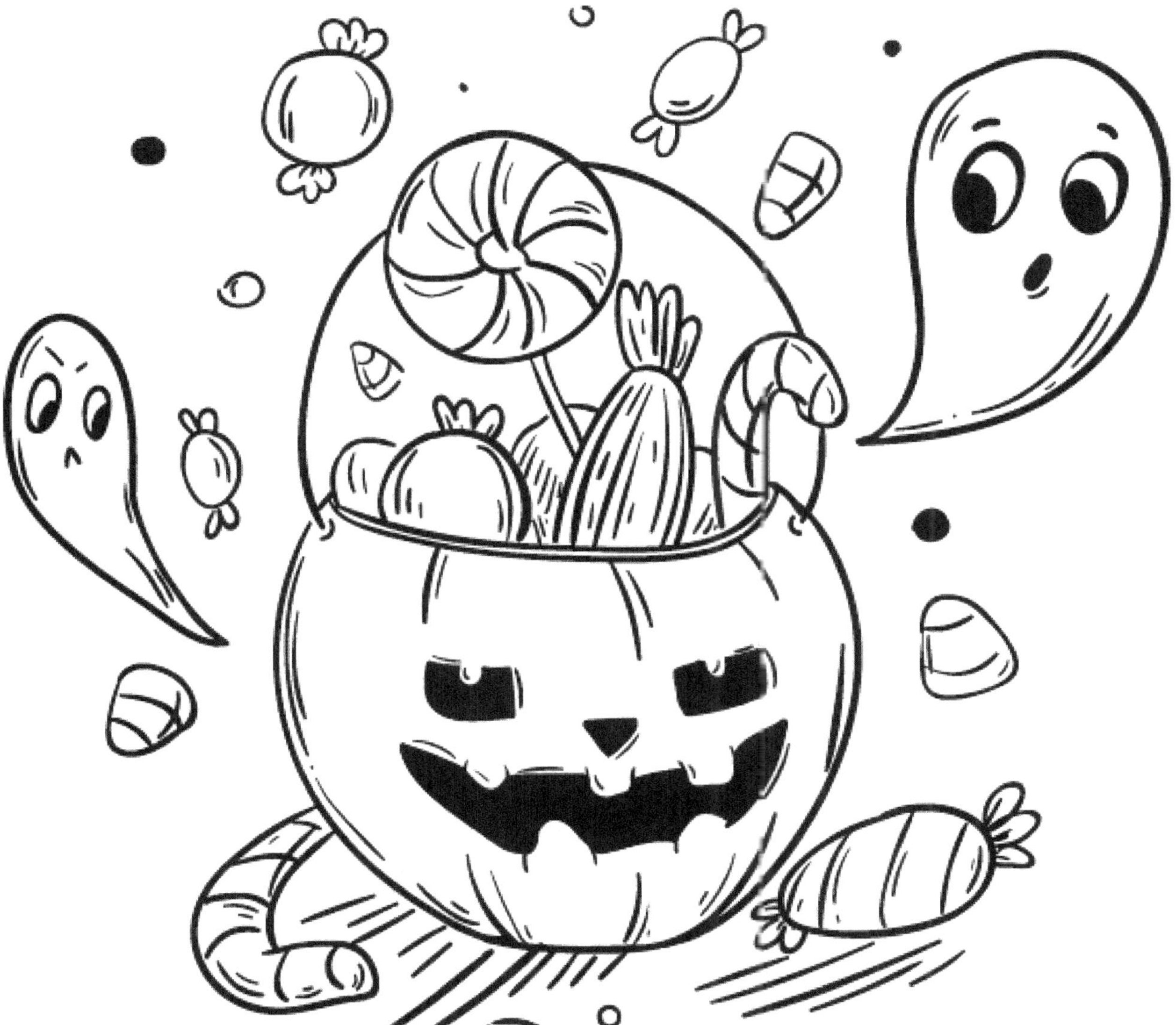

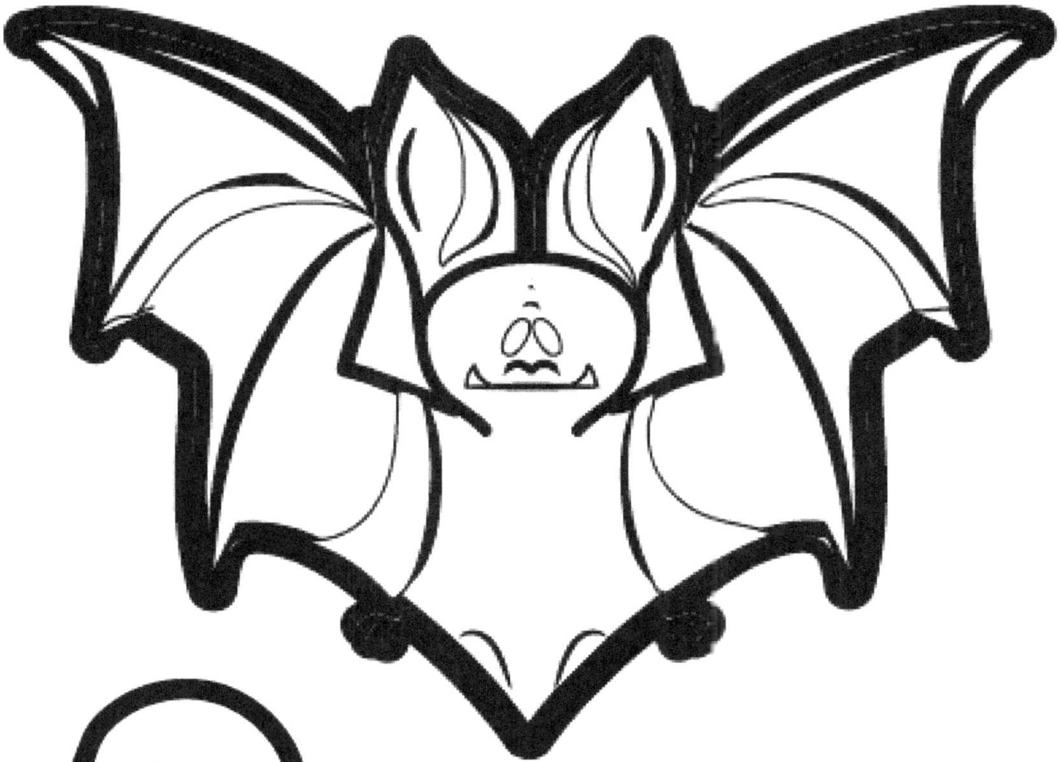
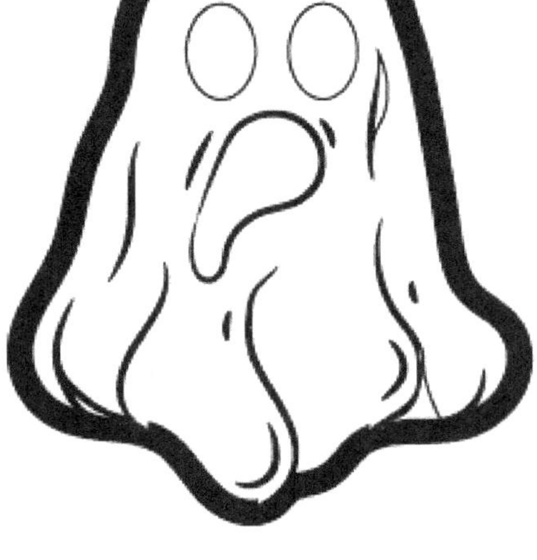
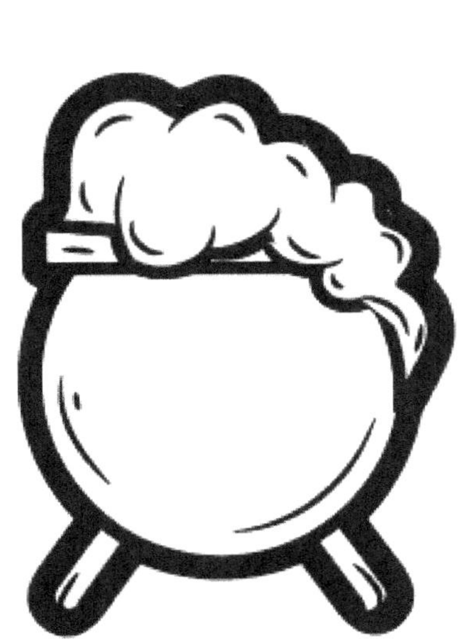
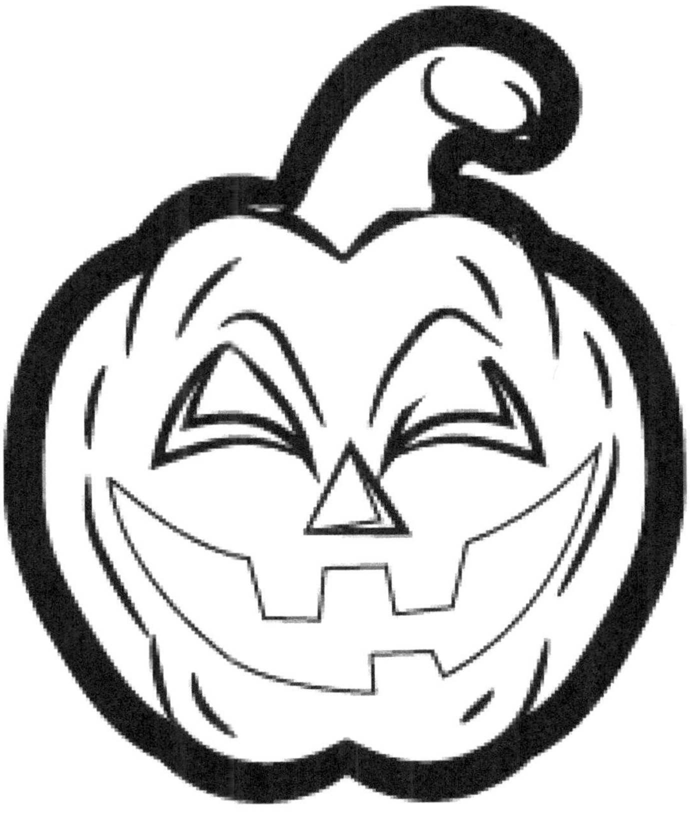

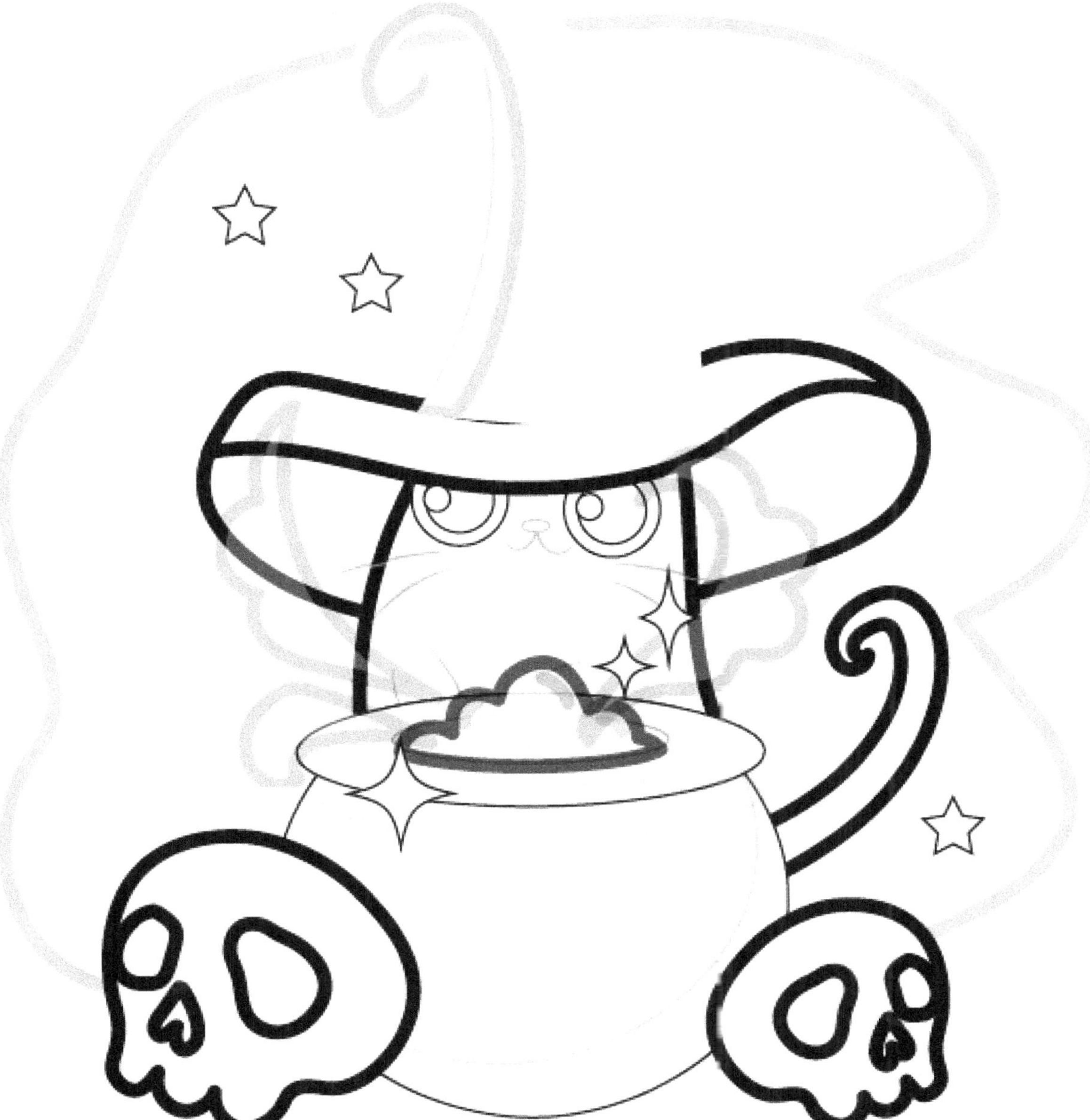

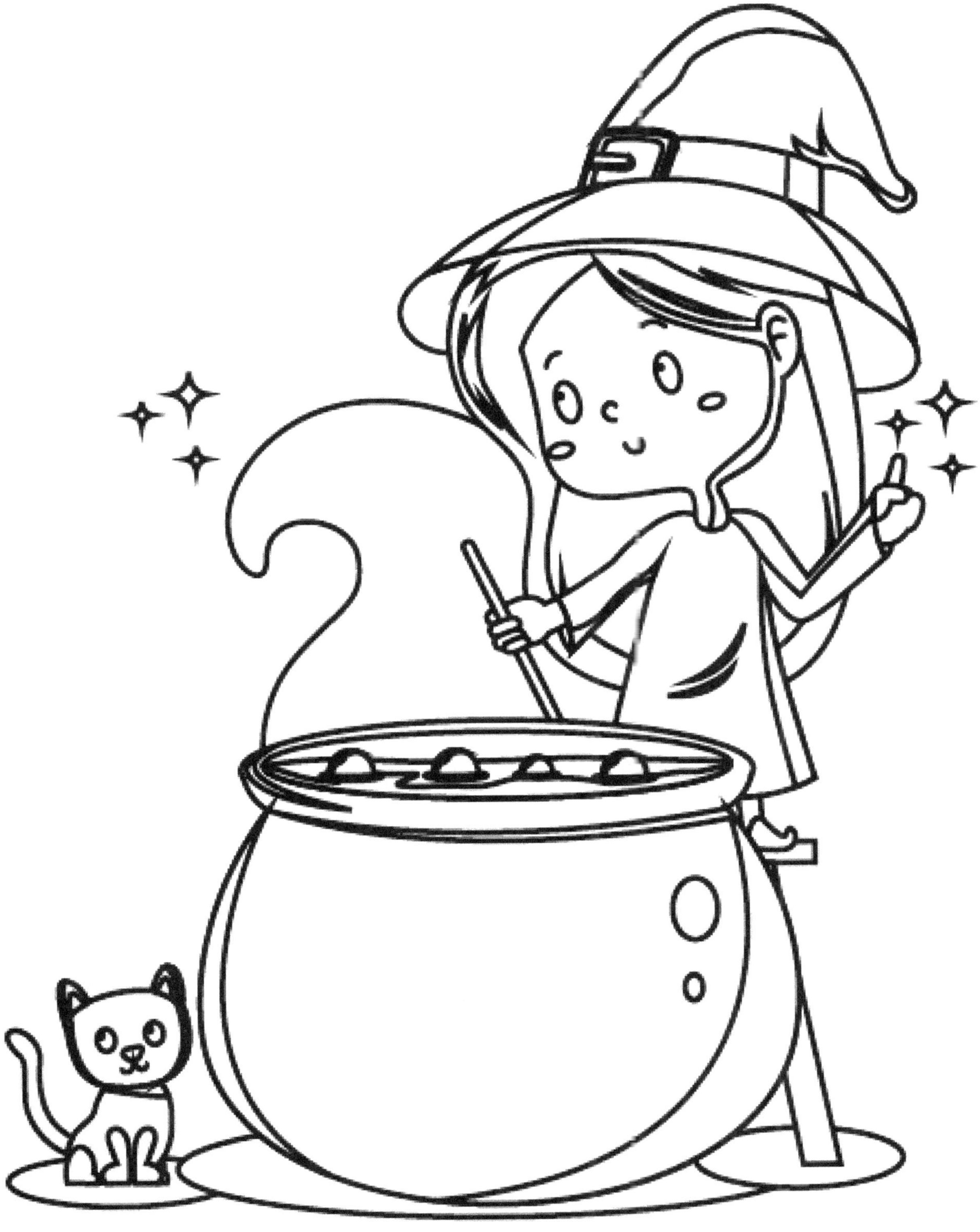

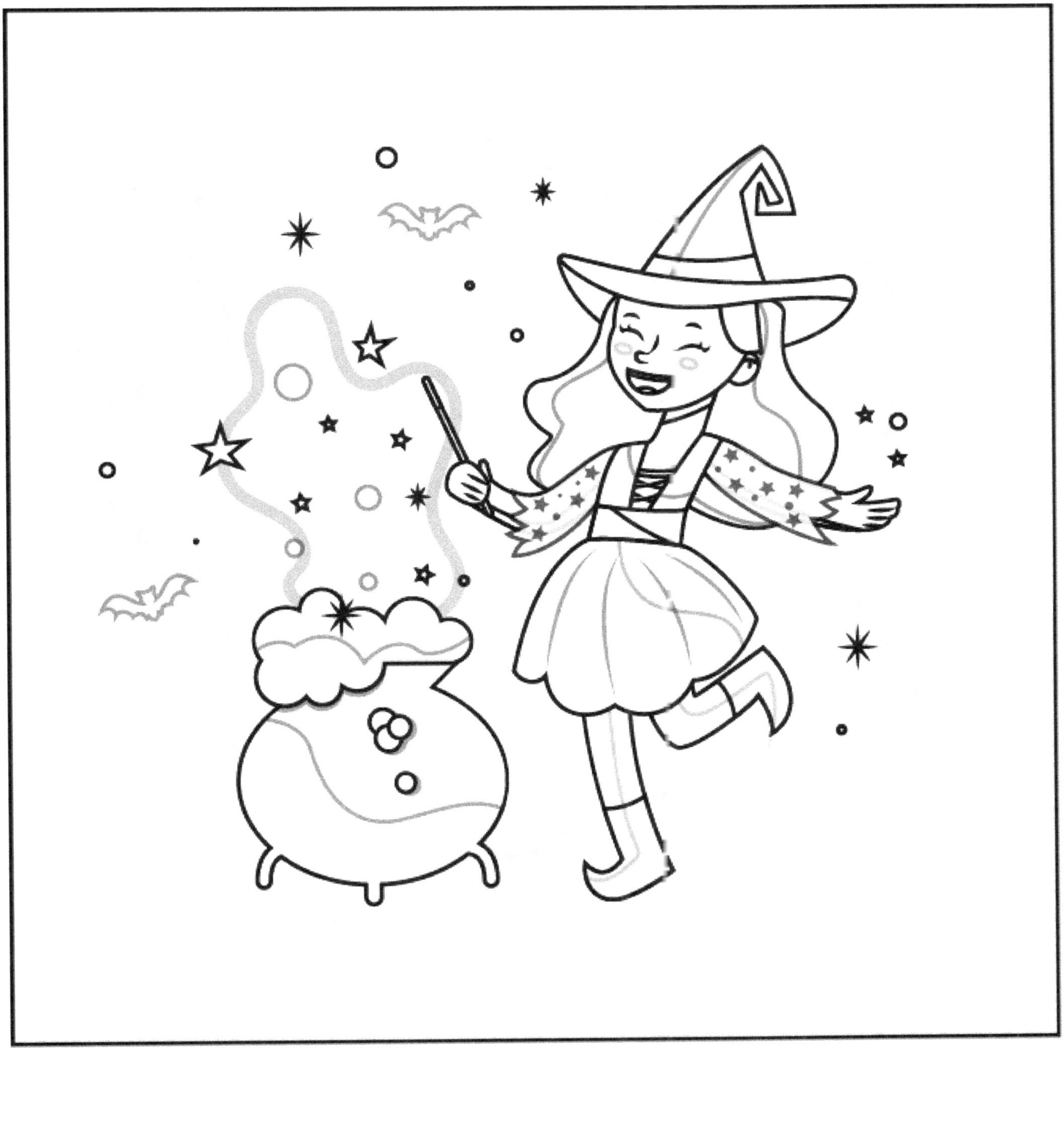

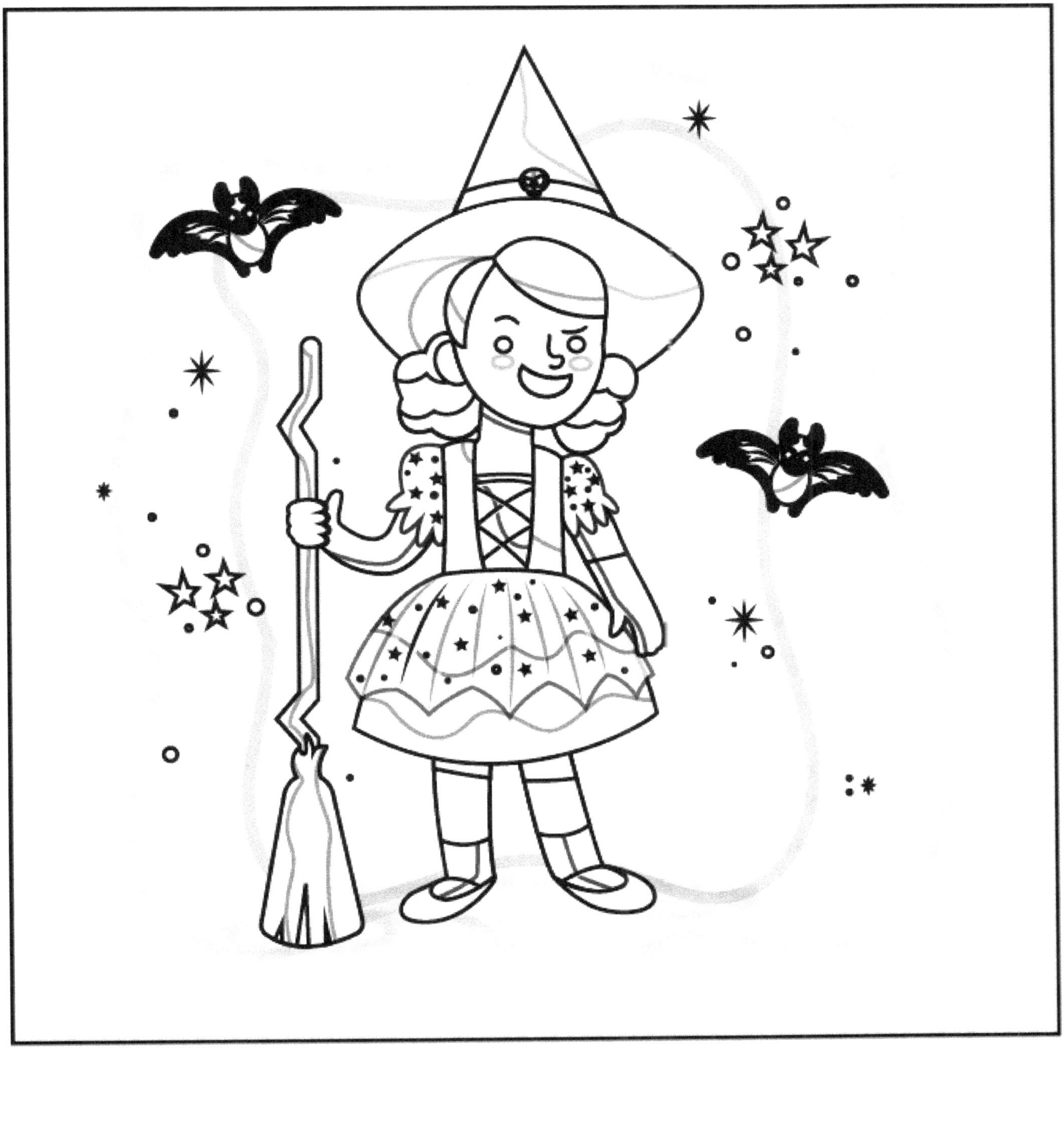

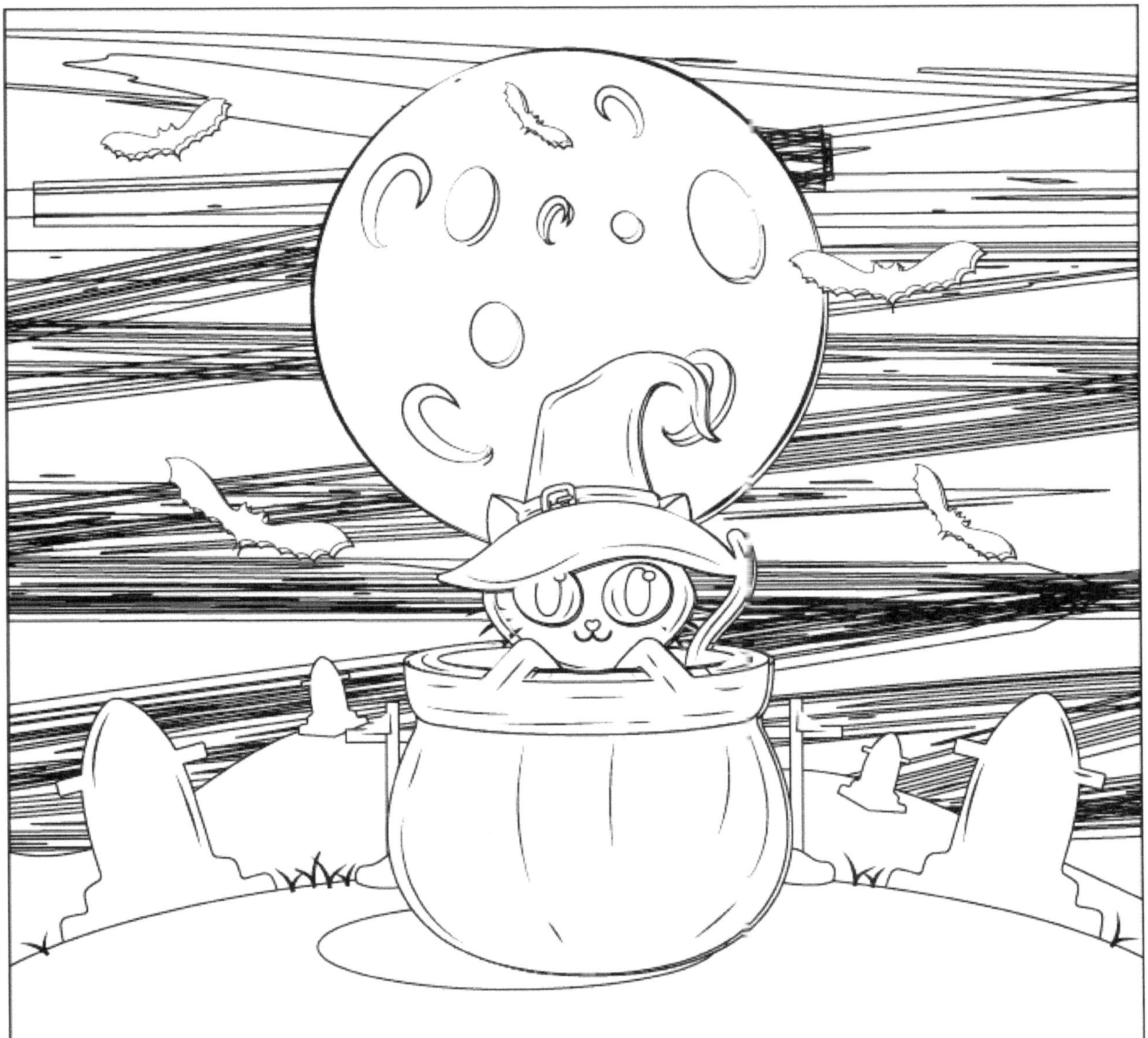

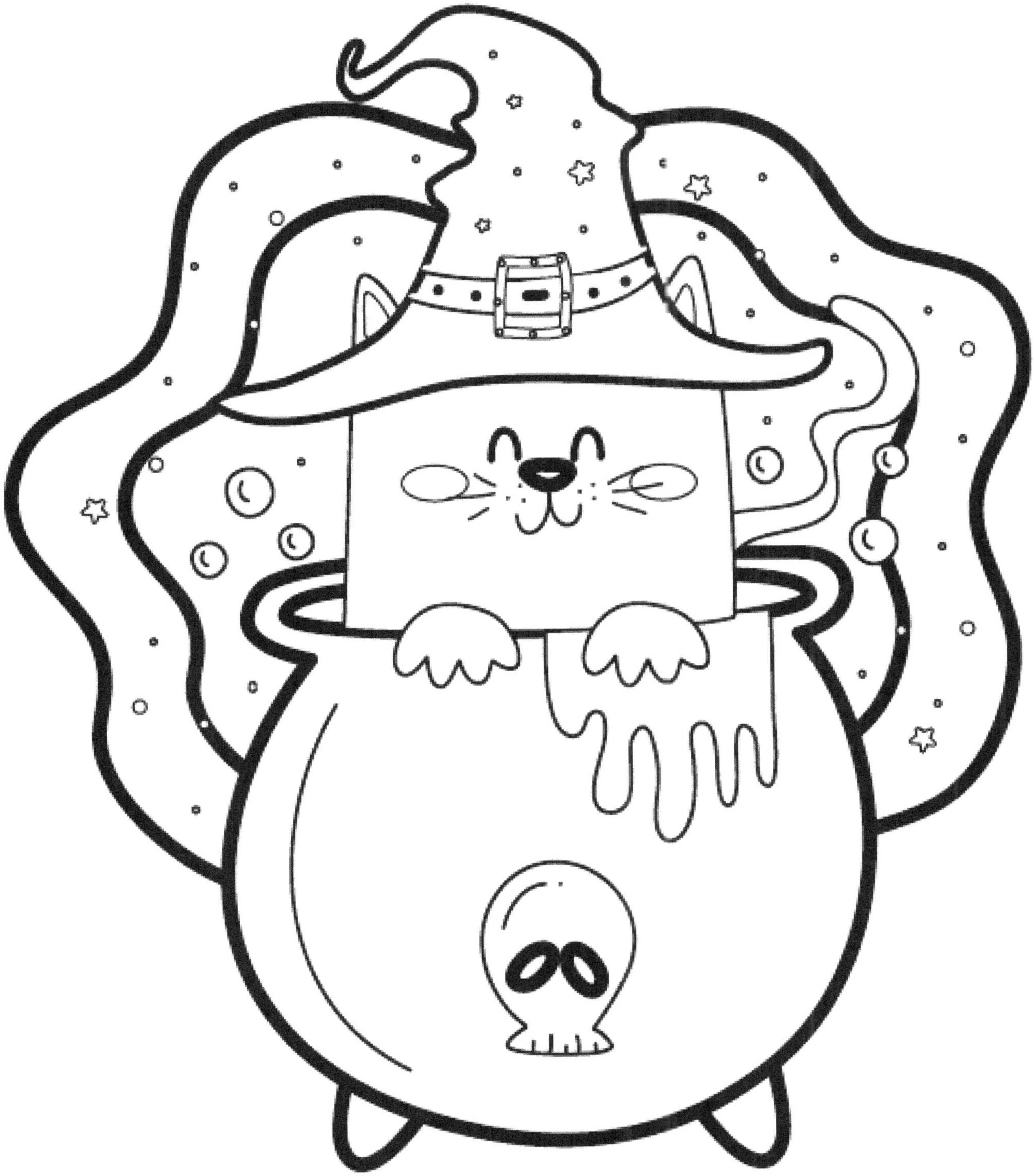

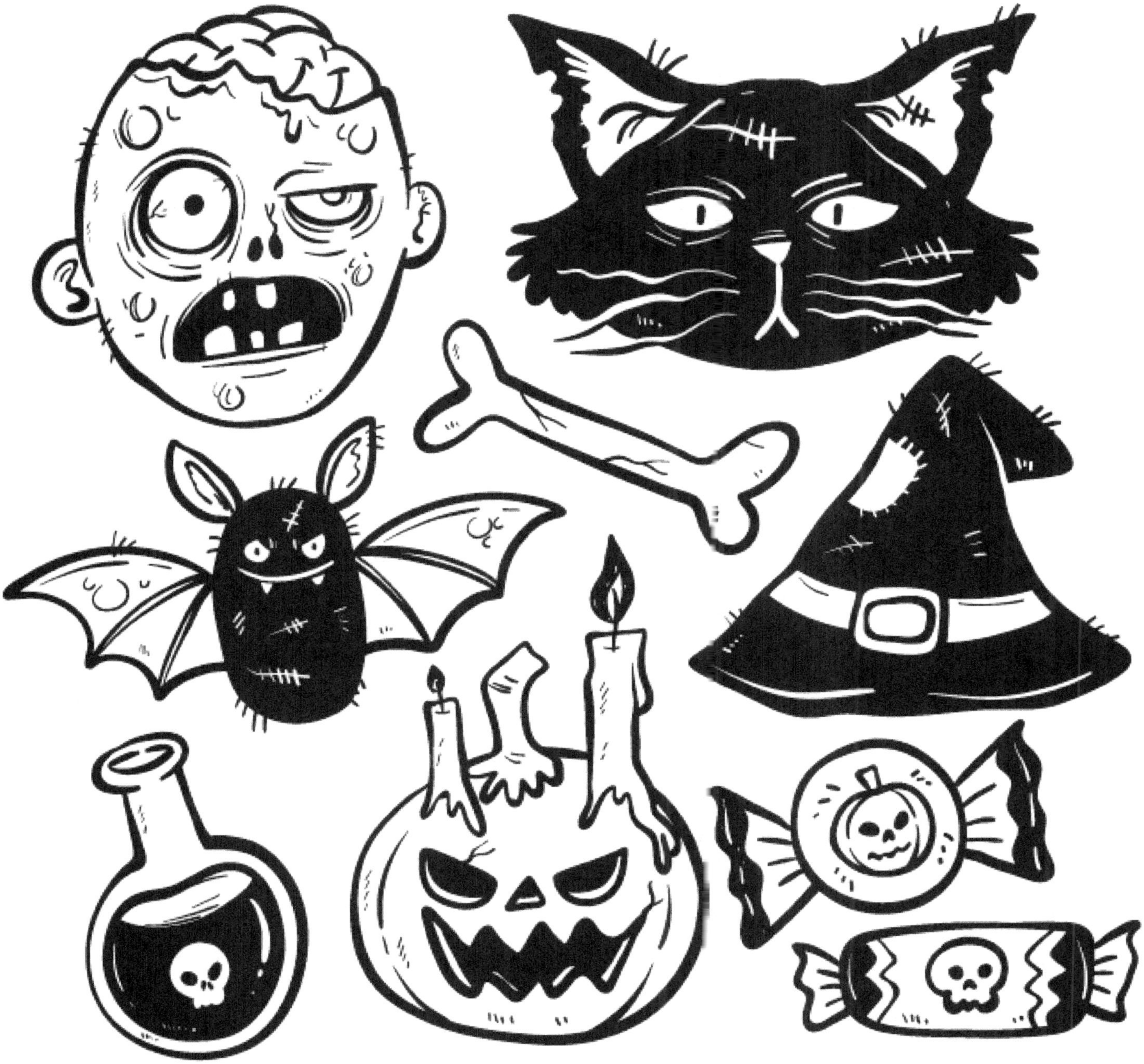

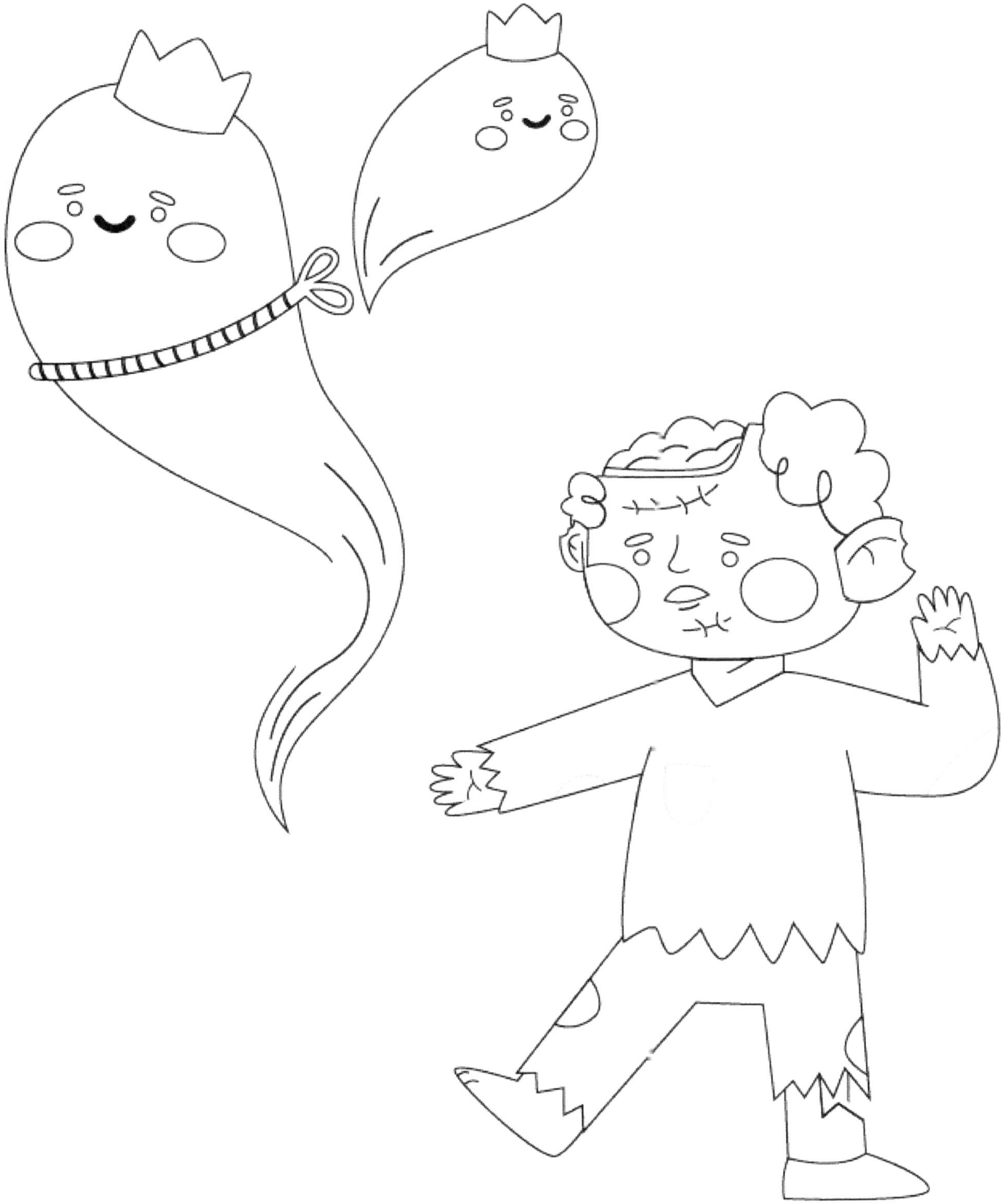

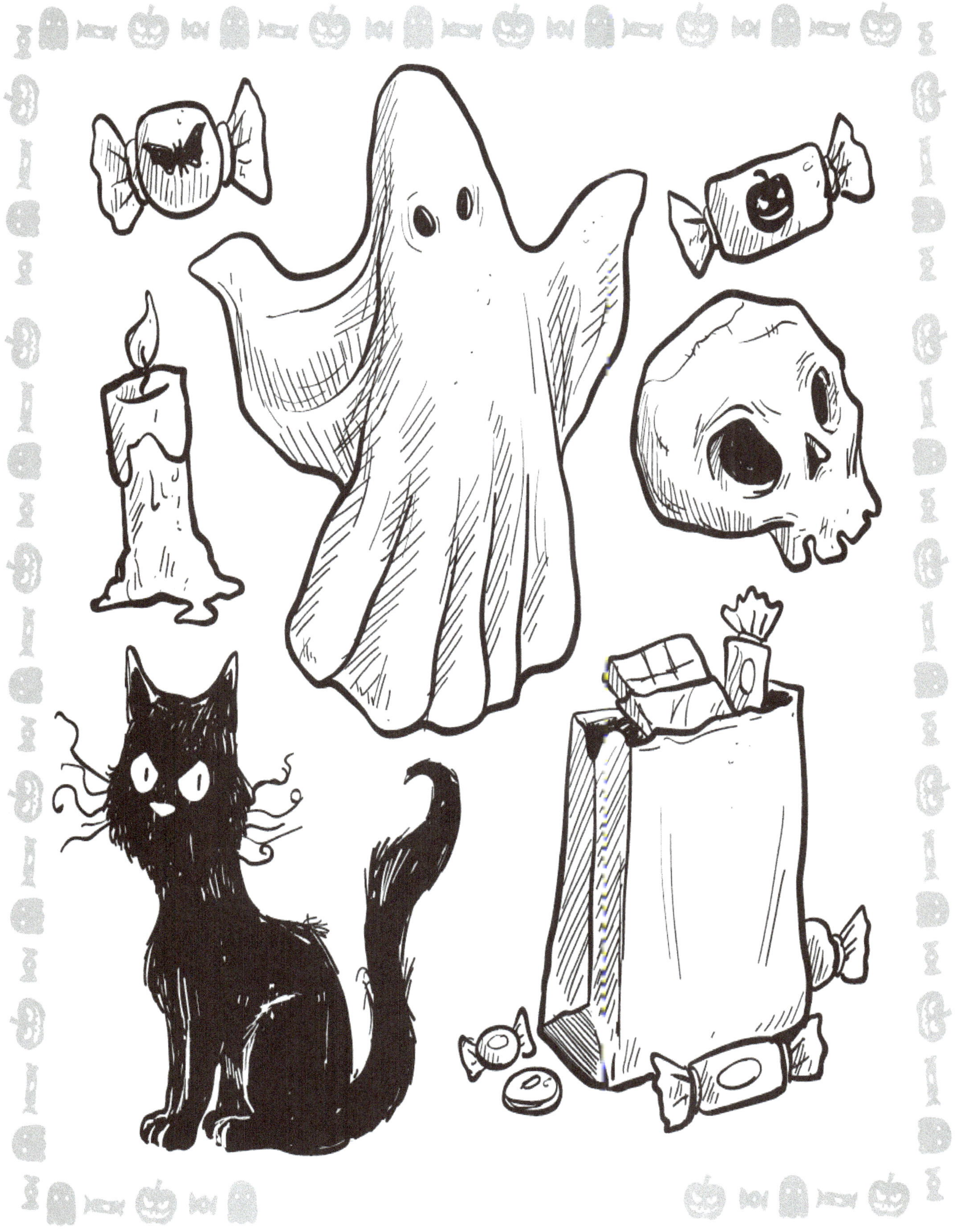

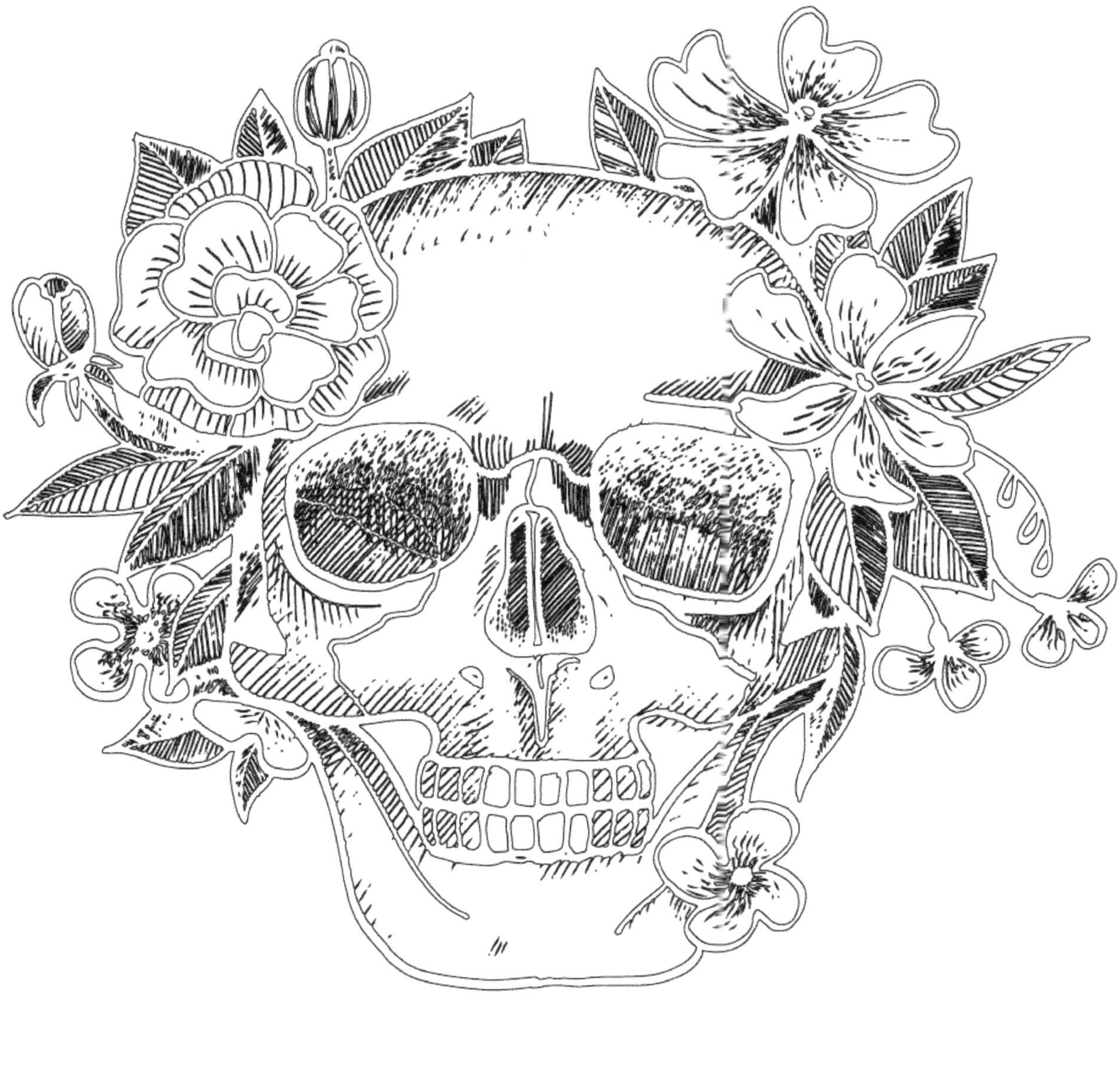

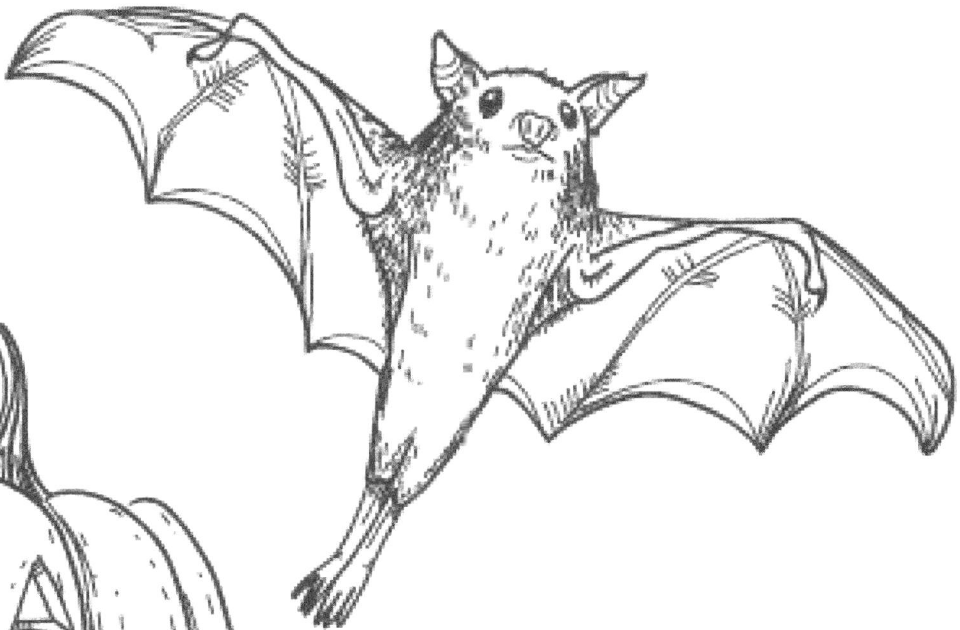

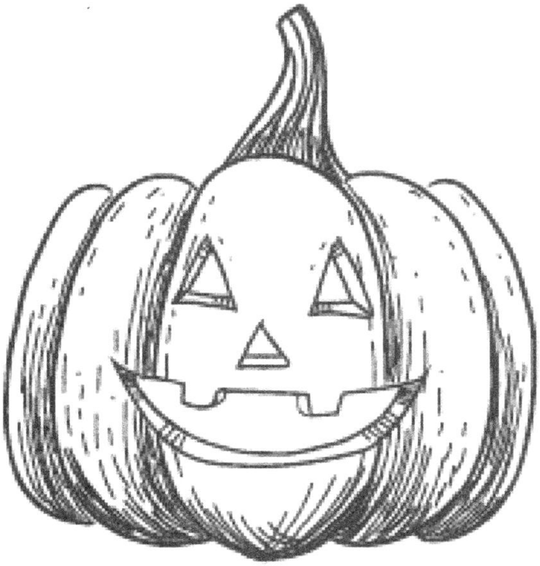

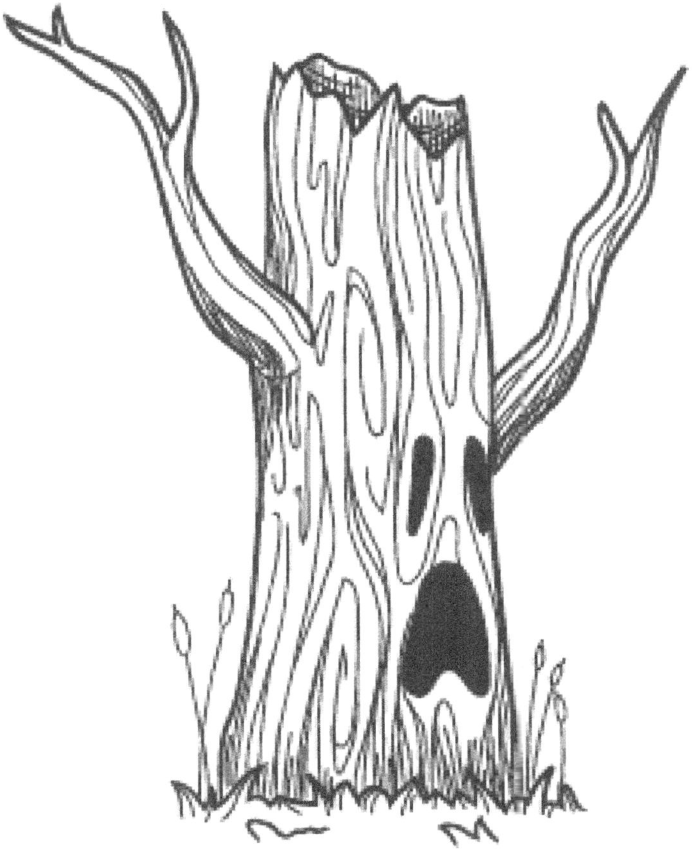

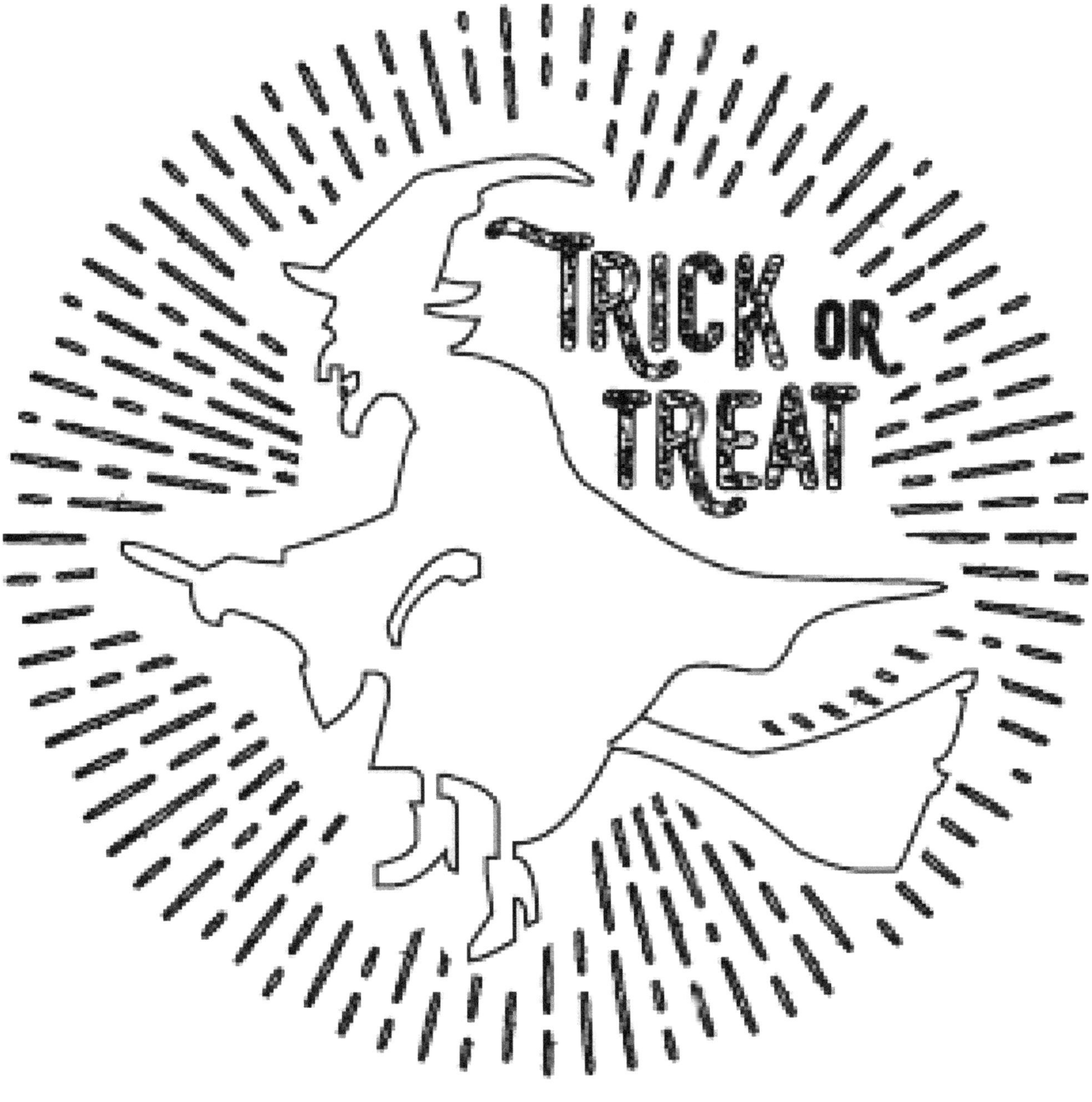
TRICK OR
TREAT

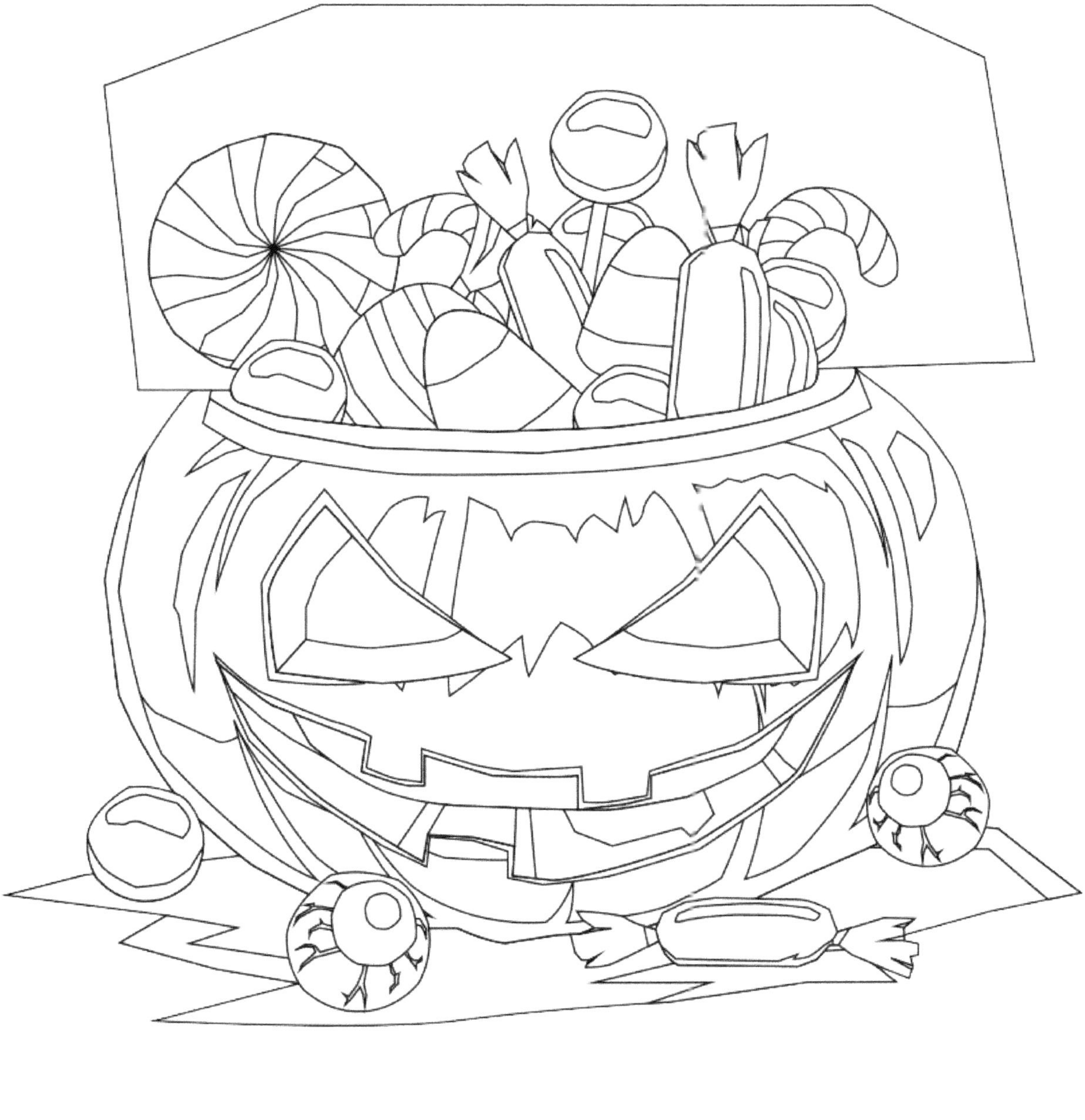

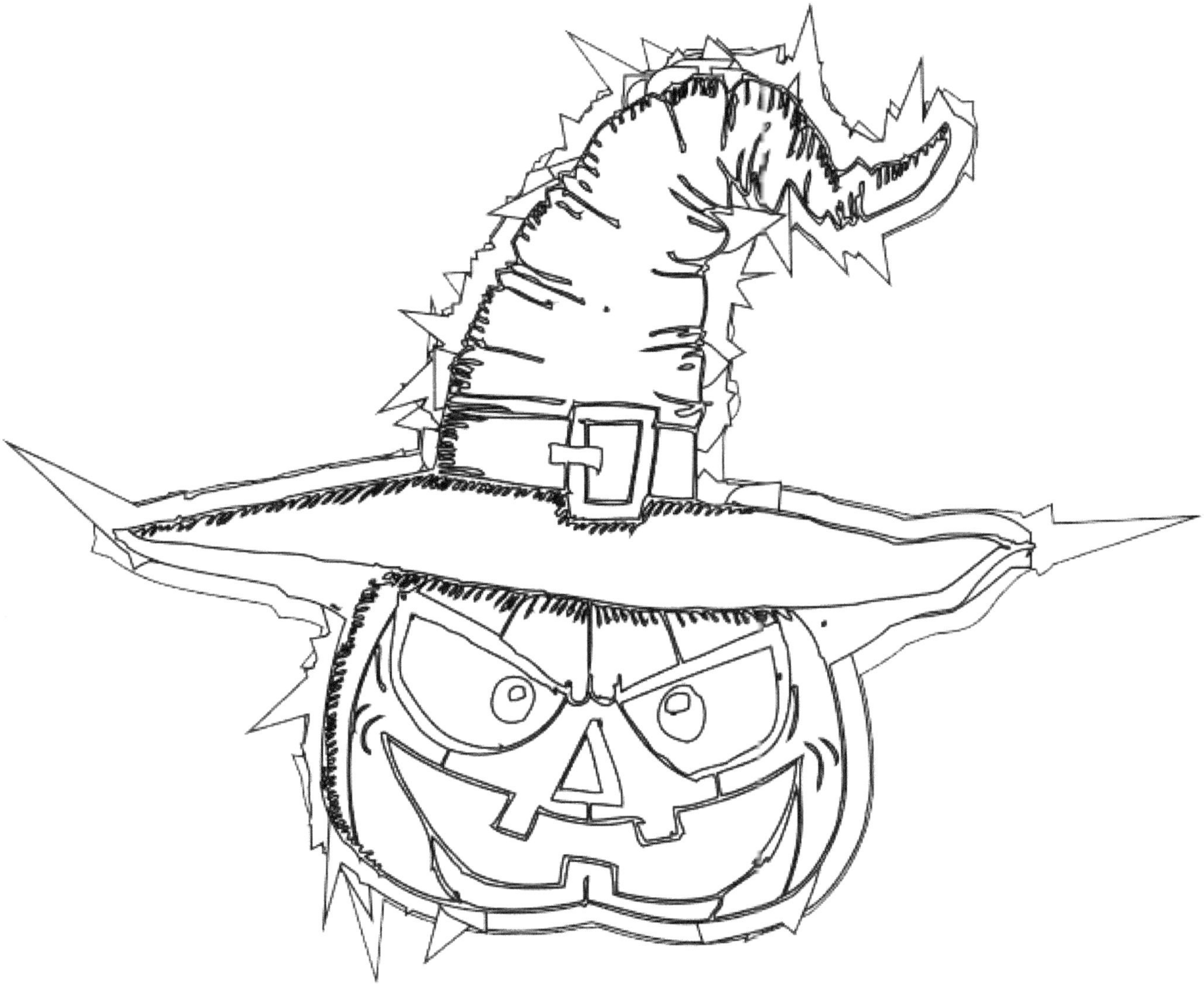

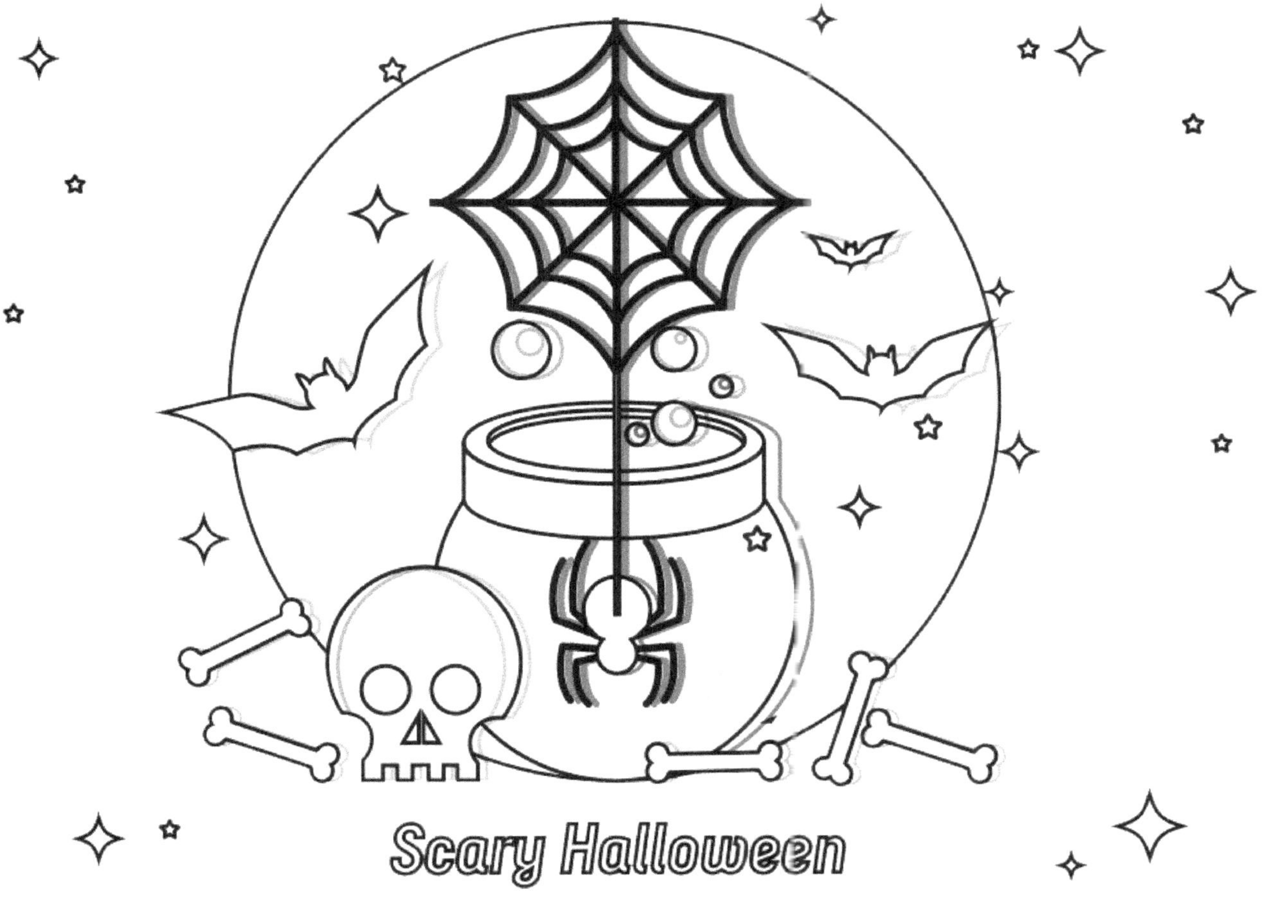
Scary Halloween

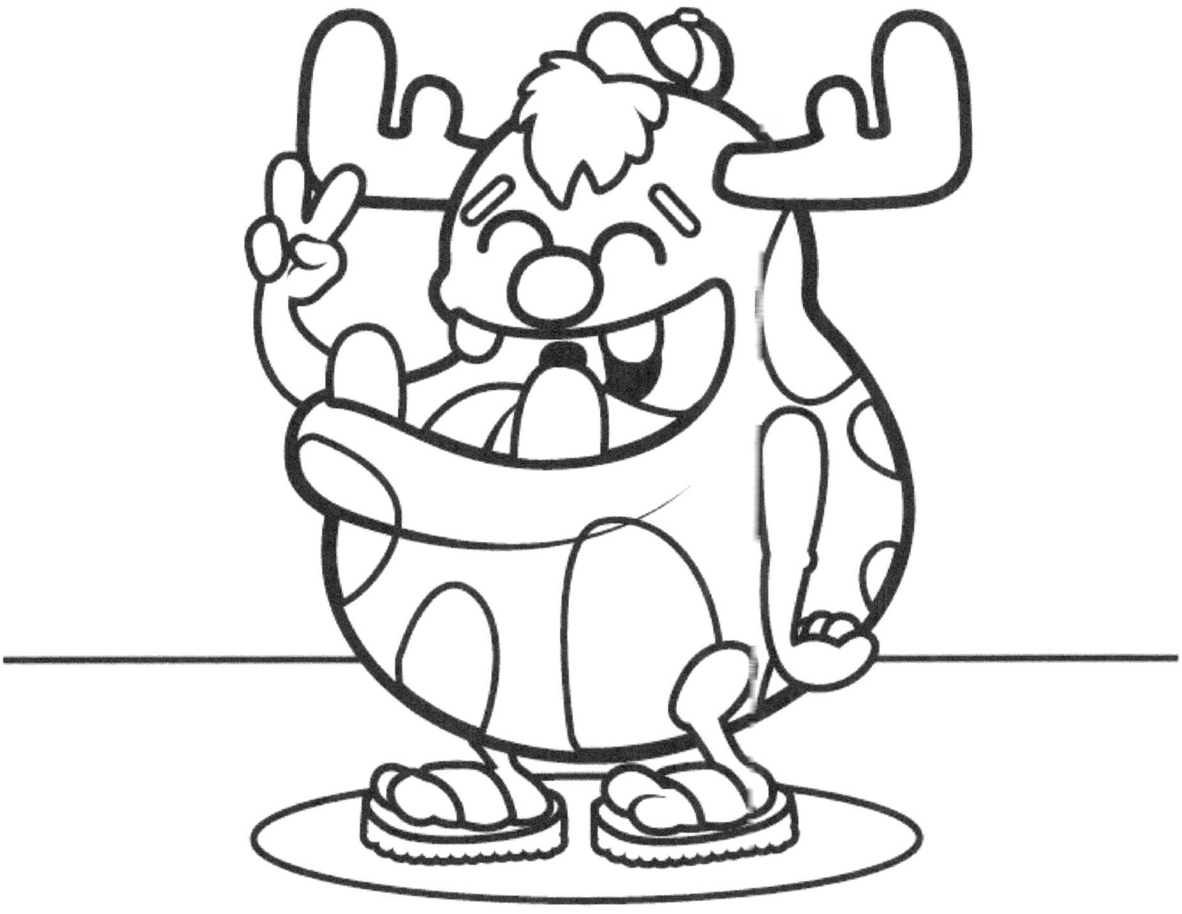

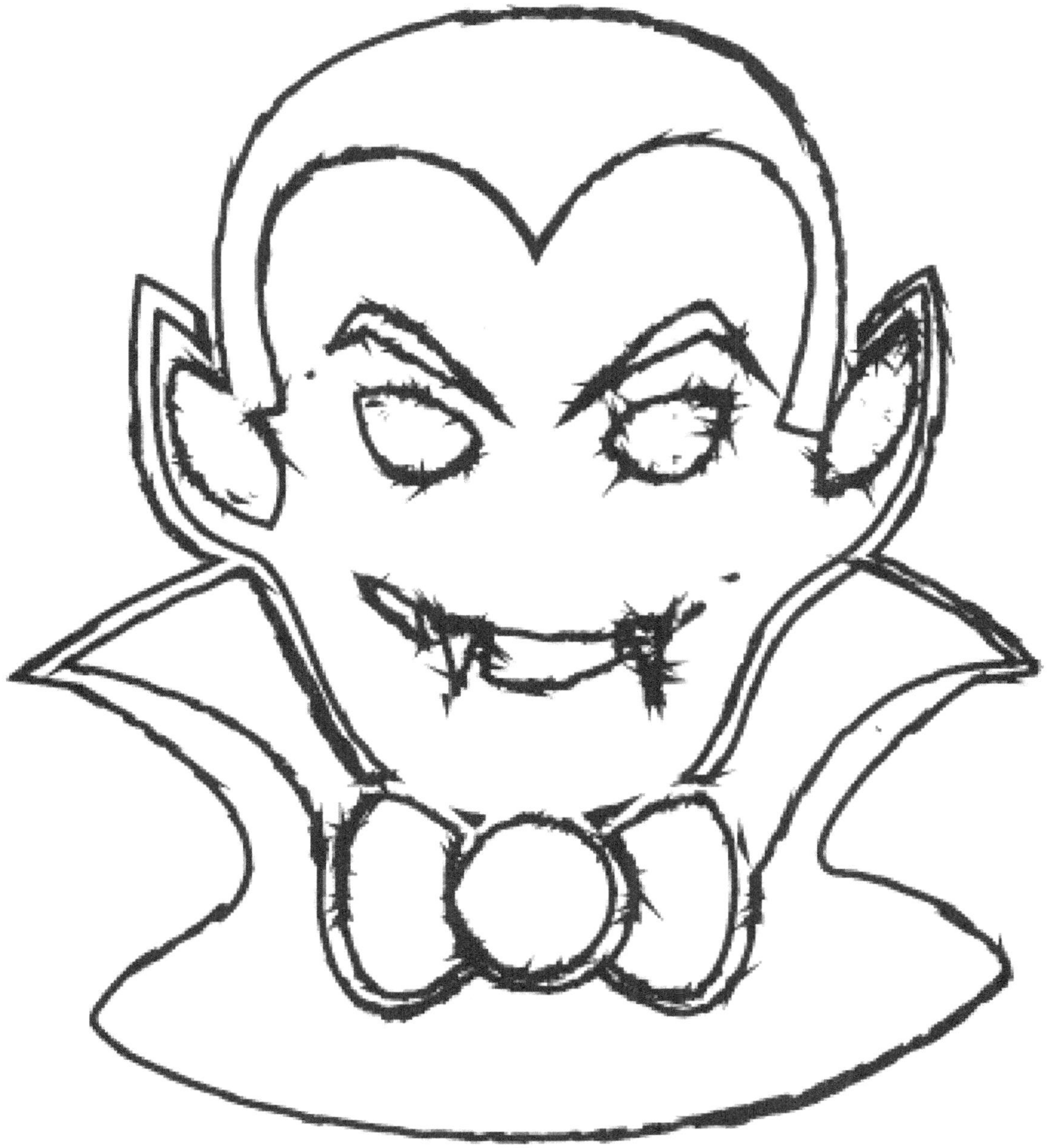

www.ingramcontent.com/pod-product-compliance
Lightning Source LLC
Chambersburg PA
CBHW060434220526
45465CB00008B/3132
9798679446304